Kamdesh

ETTs of Task Force Phoenix
Nuristan Province
Afghanistan
September 2005

James F. Christ

Battlefield Publishing

Kamdesh: by James F. Christ

Production Copyright © 2010 by Battlefield Publishing. Text Copyright © 2010 by James F. Christ. All rights reserved. No part of this book may be reproduced or transmitted in any form or by any means, electronic or mechanical, including photocopying, recording, or by any information storage and retrieval system without permission in writing from the publisher.

Cover design by Scott Lewis

For information address:
1111 North Mission Park Blvd #2031
Chandler, AZ 85224

ISBN 978-0-9788604-6-2

"Valuable historic work. Excellent job…Thanks for some very interesting insight. The official Army needs to add these pieces to their compendium on the GWOT (Global War on Terror). Well done." Former Marine Captain Dale Dye, actor (Platoon, Band of Brothers) and author (Laos File, Platoon, Duty and Dishonor).

Acknowledgements

A grateful thank you to the soldiers who served on the Kamdesh mission:

Captain Marc Oles
1st Sergeant (then SFC) Don Longfield
Staff Sergeant Scott Strate
Staff Sergeant James Dawson

Without the interviews of these four soldiers, the story behind the Kamdesh debacle would never have surfaced. And without James Dawson's personal journal, this book couldn't have been written.

Also, a grateful thank you to:

Lieutenant Colonel Patrick Coen
1st Sergeant (then Staff Sergeant) Mark Combes.

Their views of the events seen from the BDE level brought to light a perspective to the story not seen.

I would like to thank Sohee Chung, who believed in the project and was a big help with editing as well as Nick Mongiovi for preparing all of my rough drafts.

I would like to thank my friends Maurice McSorely, Marty Boetel, Andrew Robles, Morgan Neville, Jeff Angle, Tony Leach, and Sue Stein.

I would like to thank Julie Boswell for her spiritual help over the last few years during the writing of these books, and Lisa Johnston and her sister Gina Seacat, for all the help they have given me with my sons Nolan and Trace over the same time frame. I would like to thank Annette and Doyle Madsen and Maja Aleksic for being so good to my sons as well as the wonderful staff at CTA Goodman Elementary School, specifically Anna Pfau, Kay Ryan, Brooke Sawyer, Amanda Douglas, Darlene Denardis, and Maureen Sniff, for everything they've done for my boys.

I would also like to thank my family members who were and are a constant support: Joe Christ, John Anthony Christ, Brian Christ, Jeri Christ, Mary Ellen Christ-Anderson, and Gary Anderson.

Lastly I would like to give the most thanks to four people who have been my constant support no matter what the situation: my brother John Joseph Christ, my best friend Jay K Templeton, and my always-supportive mother and father, Peggy Ann Christ and John Michael Christ.

To my sons Nolan and Trace, the best gifts God has ever given me, I hope you enjoy reading about these brave soldiers. I wrote these books for you.

And lastly, I would like to thank the Lord God for all He has done for me.

INTRODUCTION

In September 2005, news telecasts worldwide reported that the Afghan National elections were in danger of being compromised. ACM (Anti-Coalition Militia) had stolen a number of ANA (Afghan National Army) uniforms and, posing as Afghan National Army troops, had moved in and stolen official ballots from a Nuristan polling site in the village of Kamdesh.

"Unless the government sends us reinforcements from Kabul," said provincial governor's spokesman Abdul Wakil Atak to Agence France—Presse, "we will not be able to conduct the elections in Kamdesh district. If there are no more troops, there will be no elections."

With the world watching, it was important that democratic elections be maintained in the country. A compromise of the elections would result in considerable embarrassment for the US and its Coalition allies who were trying desperately to establish Democracy in both Iraq and Afghanistan.

With more than 30,000 ANA soldiers and 40,000 Afghan National Police spread throughout Afghanistan (along with 15,000 American troops and several thousand Coalition soldiers) and so much obviously at stake, there was little doubt sufficient force would be sent to Kamdesh to ensure the legitimacy of the National elections.

Afghan Defense Ministry spokesman General Mohammad Zahir Azimi verified that ANA troops were being deployed to Nuristan and stated on September 12, 2005, "We will consider all possible ways to send troops to Kamdesh."

However, by September 16, there were still no troops positioned in Kamdesh. At that time, Afghan President Hamid Karzai ordered his generals to send ANA troops into Nuristan to secure the polling site. To assist, although Nuristan was not an area where American forces (or coalition forces) operated, US troops were also deployed to accompany the ANA and provide an American presence. Who ultimately gave the

order for the mission to proceed is not known, but five American soldiers accompanied the ANA into remote Nuristan. On September 23, 2005, the operation was hailed a success.
Here is what really happened ...

Kamdesh
James F. Christ

Psalm 22:11
Be not far from me; for trouble is near; for there is none to help

"Soldiers and officers alike should read these notes and seek to apply their lessons. We *must* cash in on the experience which these and other brave men have paid for in blood."

General George C. Marshall

"When the SF (Special Forces) told me they didn't go there, I'm thinking, here are elite forces, trained to do the hardest jobs in the world...and they won't go there; a whole Alpha section of SF won't go, and I am; a National Guardsmen on active duty. What sense does this make?"

> Staff Sergeant Scott Strate
> Indiana National Guard
> 34th Kandak, 1st BDE,
> 201st Corps, ANA

ASADABAD
September 12, 2005

"Sergeant Strate, Sergeant (Midwest), your mission is to proceed up to Bari Kowt with a company of ANA. You will then push on up to Kamdesh by September 16 and secure the parliamentary elections there. Do you have any questions?"

"Where are my orders, sir?"

"I just gave them to you."

"Yes, sir, but where are my written orders. All you gave me was a verbal."

"Those are your orders. Sergeant Strate, you and Sergeant (Midwest) are to proceed to Kamdesh by September 16 and secure the elections there."

"Colonel," said Strate, taken aback, "It don't work that way. Where is my mission statement? Where is my Ops Order and everything else?"

"That's it."

"Sir, it don't work that way. I been in too damn long to know it don't work like this."

"You have your orders, sergeant, carry them out."

Sergeant Scott Strate (age 34) of Richmond, Indiana, was an Indiana National Guardsman assigned to the 34th Kandak/1st Brigade/201st Corps, Afghan National Army (ANA). Strate was a 5'

10", 180 pound brown-haired, brown-eyed Steelworker with twelve years in the Guard. Presently serving in Afghanistan as a soldier/advisor, Strate was the NCO mentor to an ANA 1st sergeant. Their company had just been given a mission to proceed to the village of Bari Kowt in Kunar Province where they would continue to Kamdesh in Nuristan Province. They were to monitor the local elections and provide security in Kamdesh and its neighboring hamlets. National elections were coming up on September 18, 2005, and there was great fear the election would be compromised.

Anti-Coalition Militia (ACM) had dressed up in ANA BDUs (Battle Dress Uniforms) and moved into a polling site where they stole a significant number of ballots. The governor of Nuristan phoned the President of Afghanistan, Hamid Karzai, and told him without an ANA presence no one in his province would vote. Knowing this threatened the democratic elections of his nation, Karzai immediately phoned the Coalition governments, their high command, and his own generals to take immediate action to save the National elections.

At 0800, September 12, 2006, with the elections six days away, Strate and Midwest began passing the orders to their ANA counterparts, who in turn issued them to their Afghan soldiers. They were loading the trucks with all the essential supplies, equipment, and ammunition they would need for the operation.

Sergeant Midwest[1] was an E-7, the highest ranking ETT on the mission. He and Strate were the only Americans attached to the ANA Company. Although he wasn't an officer, because of personnel shortages among ETTs throughout the theater, Midwest was the officer mentor to the ANA company commander. He handled all the "officer" affairs in the company and Strate handled all the NCO issues.

Although a 110-man ANA company was designated for the mission, because of excessive AWOLs and a few sick calls, only thirty-eight ANA soldiers out of 110 were present. They made up the Weapons Company of the 34th Kandak, 1st BDE, 201st Corps. The Weapons Company was under the command of a Kandak (battalion) commander, an ANA lieutenant colonel (LTC).

In fairly short order Strate and Midwest had their HMMWV loaded with supplies and ammo. The ANA had done the same with eight Ford Ranger pickup trucks. Although Strate anticipated communications problems in the mountains, he and Midwest had only basic commo including a tactical satellite (TACSAT) radio in their HMMWV, an Iridium phone, and two Thuraya phones which the two ETTs distributed between them.

Strate was pleased to be finally heading out on a mission in a HMMWV (Highly Mobile Multipurpose Wheeled Vehicle). Everything he had done prior to this mission had been in a Ford Ranger. Rangers had been used with the 76th BDE, but now that the 53rd BDE had taken over, the order had come from above, "Nobody will go anywhere without a Humvee."

The convoy left Asadabad and headed on a one-lane dirt road toward Forward Operating Base (FOB) Naray, the last American outpost in Kunar Province before entering Nuristan. The convoy was making good time, and Strate inwardly hoped there would be no delays. He also hoped the ANA commander wouldn't suggest they stop. That had already happened once before and had been the cause of friction between Strate and an ANA captain. On that occasion the ANA officer had spoken to Strate's interpreter (Terp), Abdul Wahid, and said, "We need to stop now and pray."

"No, we don't," said Strate to Wahid. He knew the ANA prayed up to five times a day and he always accommodated them, but this time they were on a mission with a tight timetable. Wahid translated what Strate had said and the captain fired back in Dari, which Wahid relayed once more.

"Yes, we need to stop and pray now."

"No, we don't. I aint got time to have you all bust out your mats and pray. We gotta go."

Strate could tell the ANA in his vehicle, especially the CPT, had been extremely angered by what he had said. He also knew, however, that he was in charge and they had to do what he said. Any other time he would have complied, but back then they simply didn't have time. Strate had told them they could pray in the vehicle. He hoped another conflict would not happen now.

Strate knew he was not particularly liked by the ANA officers. He had already had several run-ins with a few of them. The foremost occurred a couple of months earlier. Strate had been attached to the company recently and was training his soldiers on infantry tactics. He had been working with them for almost nine hours when an ANA CPT appeared and started telling the soldiers the complete opposite of what Strate had just taught them. Strate had turned to Wahid and said, "Who the hell is this?" Wahid explained the ANA officer was the soldiers' company commander.

"Tell him to get the hell out of here."

"I can't do that."

"You will do that or you're fired." Strate saw Wahid go pale. The job of interpreter was one of the most sought-after positions because it paid almost four times as much as a soldier made. Strate said, "Tell him, 'This ain't your job, get the hell out of my way!'" Wahid was extremely uncomfortable as he translated, and he may have softened the language but, even still, the Afghan officer went scarlet with anger before turning and moving off.

Strate thought there were some fundamental differences in Army doctrine that had to be overcome if they were going to be successful. It seemed to him that in the Afghan army the officers had the Russian and French mentality of the officers knowing everything and the soldiers knowing nothing. That was in direct conflict with the American and British doctrines with the NCOs being the backbone of the armed forces. In the American Army, NCOs conduct much of the tactical training and the officers keep to their own duties. Needless to say, this difference in military culture did not cultivate goodwill between Strate and the ANA officers he served with.

The convoy continued to FOB Naray with the HMMWV as lead vehicle. After several hours driving as fast as the one-lane road allowed, the column pulled up to the Hesco walls of the FOB. Naray was built on an old Russian outpost. Strate was driving the HMMWV with Midwest in the passenger seat. When they pulled up to the gate, they were met by an Afghan National Policeman (ANP) and an American Special Forces (SF) operative. Strate didn't expect a warm greeting but he didn't expect an angry one, either.

"Sergeant, what are you doing here?"

Silence.

Strate looked from the angry SF operative, who had posed the question, to Midwest, who looked stunned and seemed to shrink in the HMMWV passenger seat. Strate wondered why Midwest didn't answer. He was the senior NCO on the mission. Theoretically, he was in command.

"What are you doing in our battle space?" demanded the SF operative.

Strate still expected Midwest to answer, then realized the E-7 was looking at him. Strate spoke up and said, "We're on mission. We're supposed to go up to Bari Kowt for elections. We're going to meet and greet for a couple days and move up to Kamdesh to secure the polls up there."

"*What?*"

The tone was of complete disbelief.

Strate knew he hadn't stuttered but he repeated, "We're moving up to Kamdesh in five days."

The SF operative looked at Strate in silence. After a few seconds he said, "We don't go there."

"Why don't you guys go there?"

"We *don't* go there."

Strate suddenly realized what the soldier was implying. It hit him like a punch. Here were the most elite soldiers in the United States military, unwilling to go somewhere he, a National Guardsman called up nine months earlier, was ordered to go.

The SF operative motioned Strate and Midwest into the FOB and got on his radio. He must have called his team leader because Strate hadn't even parked before an SF captain (CPT) and senior NCO walked up to the HMMWV.

"Why are you here?" asked the officer-in-charge (OIC), the CPT.

Strate expected Midwest to speak up, but the E-7 just looked to him again.

"We are going up to Kamdesh," said Strate, "to secure the polling sites up there."

The CPT looked as stunned as the guy at the gate had been.

"Why weren't we informed of this? Why are you in our battle space without orders?"

"I don't know, sir," said Strate, surprised himself that no one at BDE had told the SF they were coming.

"Do you realize we don't operate in that part of the country?" the CPT said, referring to Nuristan.

Strate didn't know what to say. He hadn't known that. It didn't make him feel any better, either. Midwest looked extremely alarmed.

"Come with me," said the CPT. "I want to hear more about this mission."

The CPT and his senior NCO led Strate and Midwest into their FOB briefing room and asked Strate to tell them everything.

"Our mission," Strate began, "is to go to Bari Kowt for a few days and do a meet and greet with the elders and local police chief. We are to do some presence patrols to let the village know that the ANA are there to help. After that, we are to head up to Kamdesh by September 16 and secure the polling site there."

The SF CPT was angry because nobody in either chain of command had informed them of this mission.

"Sir," said Strate, "Do you have any intel on the area we are going?"

"*Yeah*," snorted the CPT. "We have *plenty* of intel on the area." He led Strate and Midwest into their S-2 room and began to show them the considerable intelligence they had gathered about Bari Kowt and Kamdesh.

"In the area of Bari Kowt," said the CPT, "we have a list of seventy-five ACM (anti coalition militia) known to be in the area. Here are their names and pictures." The intel showed a similar amount for Kamdesh. Strate began examining the huge pile, thinking, "This is not good."

"If you see any of them," said the CPT, "let us know."

Strate finished looking over the documents and pictures—knowing he needed days to study the information he'd had five minutes to scan through—and asked the SF OIC to help them coordinate with the local Afghan cook in Naray to get rice and potatoes for their ANA soldiers for the next few days. The CPT was very cooperative and helped Strate and Midwest with their remaining mission prep. While they secured enough food and got everything they could from Naray, the CPT got on the radio and started asking about their mission. To Strate he seemed very surprised the operation was even taking place.

With everything they could obtain at Naray packed in their vehicles, the convoy pulled out of the FOB gate a few hours after their arrival and continued on toward Bari Kowt. Strate and Midwest didn't talk much during the drive. About the only thing said was offered by Midwest when he said, "We shouldn't be here. This is an SF mission."

They made the hour-long drive without incident and pulled into the border police base just before dusk. They set up camp for the night right outside the seventeen-foot walls of the fortress-looking Bari Kowt police station. Strate noticed that someone had written (in their best attempt at English) "Welcom ToBoder Police Bais" (Welcome to Border Police Base) on the front of the walled fort.

Strate's and Midwest's HMMWV at the Police Station near Bari Kowt.

Another view of the Bari Kowt Police Station. "Welcome to Border Police Base".

"There was absolutely no support to speak of coming from our higher...The team that was sent up there was basically told, "Hey, you're going to go. Good luck!" That was pretty much it...our joke at the time, we didn't think anybody in Kabul associated with Task Force Phoenix really had any idea what was going on outside of their walls...If it hadn't been for the Marine Corps we'd have died on the vine. We had absolutely no support what-so-ever from our own higher. We had no ammunition, no repair parts, nothing. The Marine Corps, I mean those guys stepped up and supported us. And they weren't required to. We kind of did it on the NCO to NCO level, you know; repair parts for our trucks, ammunition, food, fuel, you name it. Those guys were just great."

SSG Mark Combes
Oklahoma National Guard
2nd BDE, 201st Corps, ANA

BARI KOWT
September 13

Strate woke Midwest at 0630 so they could get organized before their meeting with the village elders. Strate had been up all night. He always took the night shift and slept while Midwest stayed with the ANA during the day. They usually worked twelve-hour shifts so that one ETT was with the ANA at all times. This morning, however, Strate wouldn't be able to rack out because they were meeting the Bari Kowt village elders for breakfast. The locals filed in and introductions were made. Everyone sat down and a breakfast of Chai Tea and rice was brought out.

From the start the meeting did not go well. It seemed to Strate that in Afghanistan, a youthful man held no position. Strate was in his thirties, and it appeared to him that unless a man was fifty or older, he was viewed as unimportant. The Afghans elders showed him zero respect. To make matters worse, Strate's Terp, Wahid, was only nineteen years old. The elders spoke to him with almost palpable distain. Strate couldn't speak either Dari or Pasto, but he knew they were being extremely unkind to the young man, who was very uneasy and constantly held his eyes down. Strate didn't need Wahid to explain to him what was wrong. He told Wahid to translate for him.

"He is speaking for me," said Strate, gesturing to Wahid. Strate had a rather intense personality. Even though he tried to be diplomatic, he was irked—so much so that even if they didn't understand English, there was probably no mistaking his tone. "An' you will listen to him cuz I don't speak your language. If you don't want to talk to him, I have nothin' to say to you."

Some of the elders appeared angered but others understood what Strate was getting at. They seemed to lower their perceived hostility level and the meeting continued. Again Strate had Wahid translate for him.

"We will be in Bari Kowt for a few days. Then we will be leaving. We will be making presence patrols and staying at the Border Police Base." Strate finished with, "We will have daily meetings to keep up communications, and that way you can let us know if you need anything."

After the meeting ended and the elders left, Strate and Midwest held a meeting with the ANA officers. They discussed what they would do next and also their intentions for the next few days. They set up observation posts (O-Ps) using the high walls of the police station so they could observe the village from all directions and had several ANA troops man each O-P. They then organized the presence patrol that would move out after lunch.

Jalalabad

Staff Sergeant Mark Combes (age 38) of Madill, Oklahoma was working in the J-Bad Tactical Operations Center (TOC) when he began hearing about what sounded like a very dangerous mission. In the last twenty-four hours there had been substantial radio traffic from Kabul concerning the operation. Higher was oscillating back and forth over the radio about how many ETTs they should send with an ANA company that was moving up to a village in Nuristan to protect poling sites during the upcoming election. As of now there were only two ETTs assigned to the mission. Higher was considering sending two more as well as some more ANA.

Combes (2nd BDE/201st Corps, ANA) was an Oklahoma National Guardsman who was a police officer in civilian life. He had been prepared to head to Iraq as a civilian contractor when his Guard readiness NCO called him from their base in Ponca City and told him he was going to Afghanistan instead.

"Man, what did you get me into?" Combes had asked facetiously even though he had always said if it came to a choice between a military and civilian opportunity, the military would get first option. That had been in February, in Oklahoma. Now, in September, Combes was an ETT in Kunar Province, Afghanistan. Although he tended to bounce back and forth between
J-Bad and A-Bad, he was presently in the former.

J-Bad was a fairly big base. It contained the Jalalabad airfield, the Marine Corps battalion HQs with some of their support people, and various other support units. There were also Afghan security force troops and some Special Ops guys as well. The ANA BDE HQ was down the road less than a kilometer away, and they were the soldiers Combes was working with on a daily basis. Across the runway was a closed compound that was "some super secret spook thing" Combes really didn't know much about.

Combes continued listening to the Kamdesh discussions. It sounded like lunacy. He wondered how they would get supplies, assets, and equipment to the troops they planned on sending because it had been hell just trying to get the J-Bad Base its necessary supplies. The mission would have to kick off soon and they had nothing to supply them. In fact, if it hadn't been for the Marines at J-Bad, Combes felt the ETTs in all of Kunar would have "died on the vine" because the base couldn't get anything from their own higher in Kabul. They needed supplies, parts for their vehicles, food, ammunition, and clothing, among other things, but they couldn't get them. Combes had learned if he needed something, after making the futile request to Task Force Phoenix (TFP) in Kabul, he'd head over to the Marines and ask them for it. They always came through even though they were under no obligation to help and could have flat out said no.

Combes listened to the continuing radio discussion and heard two more ETTs would now go (for a total of four) along with another ANA company. This was good because there was safety in numbers, but it was still a dangerous mission. It would be precarious for a platoon of US troops to go, let alone four guys. Combes felt bad for those Americans and determined to help his fellow ETTs any way he could.

Asadabad

Sergeant First Class Don Longfield (age 40) of Tulsa, Oklahoma, was an ETT NCO who had recently flown in with a company of ANA soldiers to help get a new Afghan camp squared away. The old ANA camp had been extremely primitive, so bad that an American general who had seen the conditions the Afghan soldiers had been living in ordered better, more updated facilities to be built immediately.

Longfield (1st BDE, 201st Corps, ANA) was often in the TOC making radio calls and coordinating with BDE staff. He was trying to get bids from contractors and builders to help the new ANA camp get even basic needs. He also started calling Kabul and J-Bad for supplies, equipment, and other effects. There weren't many Americans and everyone in their HQ worked closely to help each other.

While working on his own tasks, Longfield began taking radio calls for what sounded like a very dangerous mission. Being in the TOC put him in close proximity to two ETTs who had just been assigned to that mission, Staff Sergeant James Dawson (age 30) of Indianapolis, Indiana, and a major.

Dawson was a 5'9", 200 pound Indiana Guardsman. He had flaming red hair and was very likeable although somewhat eccentric. A graduate of Wabash College with a degree in history, Dawson had a somewhat caustic sense of humor. Dawson and the major, the two ETTs chosen to go with Strate and Midwest, received the mission by default. They were mentors to the Kandak occupying Camp Fyaz. Since ETTs rotated in-and-out on leave, passes, or clearing funds, whoever was organic to the Kandak staffed Asadabad missions. That was how they got assigned. Dawson had already operated for three months with the 2/3 Marines and served in places like Kandagal at the mouth of the Korengal Valley, Chow Kay, Watapoor, and Asmar. Now he would go to Kamdesh. He began trying to allocate resources for the mission.

Longfield asked Dawson about the mission. Dawson explained he had just received the assignment, had nothing allotted for it, and needed everything. Longfield said he would help. Longfield read a copy of the Tasker for the Kamdesh mission in the A-Bad TOC. The Tasker[2] included instructions to core elements on how to obtain medevac, air support, and re-supply plans, among other things. The more Longfield learned of the mission, the more he saw how difficult an operation it was going to be. He began to help his fellow soldiers prepare for it.

Longfield was working unsuccessfully to do just that when a call from higher assigned him to the mission also. He was ordered to fly to Naray on September 14 and link with a CPT Childress. Together they would await Dawson and the major, and the four would push on to Kamdesh. Longfield continued trying to acquire the assets to help them complete their mission.

Bari Kowt

At 1200, the ANA company ate rice with a few potatoes. Afterwards, Strate went over to the ANA patrol preparing to move out to make sure all the soldiers had the supplies they would need. Strate had his Terp make sure everyone knew the purpose of the patrol was to build good will with the local villagers and to show them the ANA was there to help and was not something the people needed to fear. Satisfied that the ANA were prepared, Strate ordered the patrol to move out. They left their CP at the police base and followed a road that wound several miles around the village and surrounding mountainside. Several times they stopped to speak with locals, letting them know the ANA were non-threatening. Then they moved out again. The patrol covered about four miles before returning to base several hours later.

2ND BDE HQ/201st Corps, Asadabad

Lieutenant Colonel Patrick Coen, of Mount Pleasant, Iowa, was a 5'10", 210 pound Iowa National Guardsman and an ETT battalion team chief. A former collegiate wrestler and graduate of Kirkwood College in Cedar Rapids with a degree in Education, Coen was an elementary school principal in civilian life at Mount Pleasant Elementary School.

In Afghanistan, Coen was the mentor to the ANA 2nd BDE commander. At the moment, Coen was working on several separate assignments. Although he was officially in 1st BDE, he was now attached to 2nd BDE because of personnel shortages and one recent command change.

Coen was aware of the 1st BDE mission because of all the radio chatter. He became shocked at what he heard. Several of his 1st BDE ETTs were being ordered to one of the worst places in Afghanistan.

The day before, Coen was present at a briefing where he was told the mission to Kamdesh would proceed, no matter what. His superiors said that ANA and ETT troops had to reach Kamdesh district by September 17, or the national elections would not be held in the Nuristan province—a political disaster. With reporters from all over the world watching, it was vital that democracy and the American and Coalition efforts prevailed. The mission had to proceed. So why, thought Coen, were there so few troops and ETTs designated for this mission? The powers-that-be had more troops and more firepower designated for many less dangerous areas. Coen decided to try to help get more assets assigned to the mission.

Bari Kowt

Dinner was around 1800. It consisted of rice, potatoes, and a little goat meat the ANA had purchased in the village. After dinner Strate prepared for his shift. With Wahid in tow, Strate made his first round to the O-Ps at 1900. They made sure all the ANA were alert and in position, scanning their sectors. Then they returned to the CP. For the next few hours they continued making rounds, checking each O-P.

Between rounds Strate would often talk to Wahid. The young Afghan was intelligent and personable. He spoke surprisingly good English. Wahid admitted to Strate that he and the ANA soldiers didn't know what to think about Midwest. The older ETT was likeable enough, but to the Afghans, Midwest just wasn't a soldier and didn't instill confidence like the other American NCOs they had worked with.

"Just give him time," said Strate. He didn't tell them he held the same opinion. Strate inwardly hoped Midwest would start being a better soldier because he liked him. In civilian life they'd probably be friends. In the military, however, their fellowship was trying. The only conversation they'd had that day was Midwest complaining how they shouldn't be there.

Suddenly, gunfire erupted from one of the O-Ps. It was automatic fire from an AK-47 coming from across the compound. Strate unslung his M-4 and ran to the O-P with Wahid right behind him. When they got there, Strate found an ANA sentry holding his AK. The Afghan was looking out into the night. Strate couldn't see anything in the blackness.

"Ask him what the hell is going on," said Strate to Wahid. The Afghan Terp spoke quickly to the ANA soldier, and the man responded just as fast.

"He says he saw someone in the cornfield."

"Ask him if he's sure of what he saw."

Wahid spoke again, and the soldier nodded and spoke back.

"He says he's sure he saw a figure in the cornfield."

"Ask him why he's shooting at the figure he claims he saw?"

Wahid posed the question, and the soldier responded.

"He says he was scared, so he opened fire."

Strate took out his night vision goggles (NVGs) and scanned the area in front of the O-P. He couldn't see anyone in the cornfield. Either the man was lying unseen on the ground, dead, gone, or had never been there in the first place. Strate was preparing to head back to the CP when gunfire erupted from one of the O-Ps on the other side of the compound. It hadn't been two minutes since the first shots. Strate and Wahid raced to that position. They found another ANA soldier standing with his AK.

"What's going on?" Again Wahid did the translating.

"I saw someone out there."

Strate scanned the area with his NVGs. He couldn't see anything. By now several ANA soldiers had followed them to the O-P.

Strate had Wahid tell one of them to go get the ANA non-commissioned officer-in-charge. When the NCOIC arrived, Strate reprimanded him.

"Your soldiers have to maintain fire discipline. We can't open fire on everything we think we see."

"Why not?"

"There might be local villagers out there and we might shoot them instead of the enemy."

"If they are up at night and moving around, they are the enemy."

Strate returned to the CP and called the SF to let them know about the shooting. Probably nothing was happening, but in the event it turned into the prelude of an attack, he wanted the closest help to be aware. Then Strate realized he hadn't seen Midwest. Multiple shots had been fired. Strate knew when he had heard the shots, he had grabbed his M-4 and come running, expecting the worst. Where was the E-7? Had he slept through the gunfire?

"I wanted to cancel the mission. I was told 'go' by CFC Alpha. We didn't even have an Ops order. When I questioned the lack of intel, I stated we didn't even know if we could get there. I was told they would drive as far as possible, park, and walk the rest of the way. We were told NOT to travel in anything less than the new type up-armoreds but that didn't make a difference with this mission... [Also] all 2/3 Marines were assigned election missions prior to this mission - [they were] 100% tasked! This meant no QRF...When I checked, it was "no" on fire support, a "wait" on fixed wing CAS—rotary wing couldn't reach, had to be fixed wing from Bagram—and a "maybe" on medevac stripped-out and stocked with auxiliary fuel...ETTs continued to be put in crazy places, but nothing like Kamdesh."

Lieutenant Colonel Patrick Coen
Team Chief, 2nd BTN, 1st BDE
201st Corps, ANA

JALALABAD
September 14

Captain Marc Oles (age 35) of Des Moines, Iowa, had just returned from Kabul when he received a call from LTC Coen at 2nd BDE HQ. First BDE needed another ETT for a mission to the village of Kamdesh in the Nuristan Province. Four American ETTs were escorting two companies of ANA infantry to Kamdesh, and their mission was to secure the polling sites for the national elections. Coen explained they needed more ETTs for the operation and asked Oles if he would go. Oles wouldn't be in command but he was asked to go because the major leading the mission was weak, and Coen knew Oles had a lot of operational experience under his belt. Oles willingly accepted. Coen told him to get to Asadabad ASAP because the mission was scheduled to kick off at mid-afternoon on September 16, two days away.

Oles had to move fast to catch a helicopter leaving for Asadabad. Once in the air, via radio, he talked to the mission OIC, the major. Oles told him he was en route from J-bad and asked the major to prepare specifics for him upon his arrival because he didn't have much time.

"Make sure you get radios set with the proper security fill," he advised. "We'll need maps, graphics, and background intel of the Nuristan area, especially Kamdesh and the road we will be taking in. You know, just a basic combat prep."

"Roger that," said the major.

Oles was 5'11'', 175 pounds, with black hair, brown eyes, and olive skin. He was German on his father's side of the family[3] and Korean on his mother's. Oles began his military service as a Marine. He then used the GI Bill to go to college in Des Moines at Drake University. During Desert Storm he deployed with the Iowa National Guard. When he got back, he was commissioned a regular officer and spent his entire time with the 82nd Airborne. After his service ended, he once more became a civilian and took a job as a stockbroker. He never thought of the military as a career and never planned to return to duty. But after September 11, he knew the country was at war and felt it was his patriotic duty to serve. He volunteered and joined the National Guard. From late 2003 to the end of 2004, he was the CO of a rifle company in Bosnia. He returned home December 15, 2004, and was home one day before he received orders on December 16 to go to Afghanistan.

It was now almost nine months later and he was on a helicopter heading for Asadabad.

Bari Kowt

Strate woke Midwest up at 0700 so he could take his shift. He was exhausted. He had been up for almost forty-eight hours and needed sleep badly. He remembered the gunfire from the night before and told the E-7 that the next time he heard shots, he had better grab his weapon and investigate. Strate then went over their plan for the day. Midwest was meeting with the village elders and the police chief today. Because of the two incidents the night before, Strate saw a definite need for communication with the locals before someone got killed.

"Make sure the elders and the police chief tell their villagers to stay inside after dark or carry flashlights and identify themselves as friendly." Midwest nodded in understanding as Strate added, "Call our chain of command. Check in and see if we have orders yet." With that, Midwest moved off to the CP and Strate lay down for some badly-needed sleep.

Asadabad

Oles's helicopter made the quick flight to Asadabad and landed on the LZ. Oles went immediately to the TOC and met with the major who would be leading the mission. The first thing Oles asked him for was the mission prep. The major seemed surprised and Oles was shocked to find the OIC didn't have any of it. Nothing had been done. The major had failed to follow through on even one of his requests.

Oles immediately set to work to get everything his unit needed, but he found it was an uphill battle. He needed support, intel, and orders for the mission. He couldn't get anything from 1st BDE/201st Corps, the BDE his mission was assigned to. With no luck getting an Ops Order or any kind of paper trail, Oles went to meet with his NCOs and discuss the situation with them. However, only one of the three NCOs who would accompany him on the mission was there—Dawson.

Dawson's involvement was good! Oles had worked with Dawson before during a tour in Bosnia over a year earlier. They were both Indiana Guard. More recently, the two had worked a checkpoint in Kunar only months before—"Doghouse", a battery of 105s able to support many of the surrounding FOBs. Oles respected Dawson's ability and knew the SSG was a competent and proven asset.

Oles asked Dawson if he'd been able to acquire any of their needed support for the mission. Dawson said he'd been unable to get anything from anyone. Oles asked where the rest of his NCOs were, and Dawson told him the other two were supposed to be waiting at Naray. (They hadn't been informed that Strate and Midwest had moved up to Bari Kowt.)

At 0800 Longfield was waiting in the TOC for word about an arriving helicopter. He was expecting a flight heading for Naray. He was supposed to go up early and link with CPT Childress and then await Dawson and the major. After half an hour the helicopter had still not arrived. Then Longfield received a radio call from higher telling him he wasn't going on the mission and that no ETTs were. Shortly after that, another call came informing him that Dawson, Oles, and the major would go. Longfield felt the conflicting message was nothing out of the ordinary and simply typical of the way Army orders constantly changed.

Longfield began assisting Oles, Dawson, and the major with the prep of the HMMWV, loading equipment, stocking up on MREs (Meals Ready to Eat) and water, and getting their radios ready. While everyone who was preparing to depart worked on their own responsibilities, Longfield kept hearing the senior American officer assigned to the mission (the major) repeat earnestly how he really wanted to go on the mission. However, behind the scenes Longfield noticed the major doing everything he could to avoid going. This had been going on since the 13th, when the major initially tried to get the mission cancelled outright. When that failed, he began attempting to maneuver so that he would have to stay behind. Dawson picked up on this, too, as did the newly-arrived Oles.

No one thought the major would have any success sliding out of the mission. For one, it had to proceed; and two, they were already so short in numbers, they felt there was no way anyone would be left behind. If anything, they needed more men.

Longfield knew what an extremely dangerous mission this was to send so few Americans on. He felt the operation was hazardous in every way. Because Longfield recognized more bodies would be needed, he radioed Coen, his battalion team chief, and it was determined he would accompany Oles, Dawson, and the major. Only now, with the addition of Longfield, 1st Brigade suddenly decided (with urging from the major) that the major wouldn't be needed. The major had been attempting to convince CFC Alpha—the colonel—that he needed to stay back and work on some other issues, most importantly, getting the ANA base up and running. With Longfield now a part of the team, the major had been able to lobby his point even stronger. Just like that, the major was now staying behind.

Coen was in command of the ETT advisory team. He now worked in 2nd BDE HQ and was not directly involved in the 1st BDE's mission to Kamdesh. However, when he found out the major had managed to avoid the mission, he became angered. Coen sought him out and told the major flat out, "We need you to go on this mission."

"I don't go on missions."

"You will go on this one."

"I have a bad back. I'll medical out."

Coen was disgusted. He knew the major was not mentally strong and he also knew the man was having problems at home, but this was low. Realizing the major would be a liability, not an asset, Coen didn't say anything more to try to keep him on. Oles, Dawson, and Longfield were not upset to hear the news—or surprised. Oles became the new mission CO.

Newly invigorated, the major earnestly began to help the others finish their prep.

"You know," he said to Longfield as they loaded supplies, "I really want to go with you guys."

"Sir," said Longfield, "Let's not bullshit one another. You don't want to go. It seems you're obviously scared. It's no big deal. It is what it is."

"Bullshit," said the major, "I want to go, I just…"

"Sir, you don't have to impress me. You don't have to convince me."

"I'm not afraid of anything," spat the major angrily, "I'll kick your ass!"

"Major, don't threaten to kick my ass."

"I'll kick your ass!"

"Sir, you couldn't kick your own ass."

The two argued back and forth until the major moved angrily away, giving Longfield a dirty look. When Oles walked up, Longfield turned to him and said, "You know, that major just threatened me…which was basically just asking me to kick his ass."

"Are you kidding me?"

"You know, he's not very tough, I think I could take him."

"You outta report that to the colonel."

"Nah, it won't do any good."

Longfield turned his attention to his new mission. But he still couldn't understand why they were having so much trouble getting anything for this operation.

Oles, having just arrived, was trying to get caught up. He knew Dawson was good and thought Longfield looked solid, so he didn't have any concerns with the American element; but when Oles discussed the situation with Longfield, he was shocked at what the SFC had to say.

"First, they told me to be ready to go," explained Longfield. "Then they called back and told me no Americans would be going and only ANA troops would go. Then they called a third time and told me we were going again." Longfield was a professional soldier. Orders were orders and he would follow them. But he couldn't shake the feeling that the organization for this deployment was haphazard, partly because the mission kept changing.

"They finally called again," continued Longfield, "and gave me the specifics: Five American ETTs would be accompanying the ANA into Nuristan."

Longfield knew this was not typical Army procedure. ANA rarely ever moved without a platoon of Marines or US soldiers with them, in addition to the embedded training team. It was very strange that there was no coalition ground support deploying with the ANA.

Oles absorbed the information without saying anything as Longfield continued.

"As soon as they notified me, I immediately got on the radio and began making the necessary calls to ensure we'd have close air support, medevac (medical evacuation) capability, and artillery support. But I can't get any positive answers. The close air support doesn't look promising and medevac wants no part of flying in Nuristan. On top of that, there's no arty (artillery) close enough to support us where we're going."

Longfield, being a combat veteran and having previous deployments to Bosnia and Afghanistan under his belt, was not one to get nervous. But he paused for a moment and then added, "Sir, to be honest with you, I don't have a good feeling about this mission."

Oles didn't say anything. As a commander, he couldn't. But he, too, felt uneasy. "Why can't we get an Operations Order?" he thought. They had nothing that would spell out their "Task-Purpose-Intent." All they had was the name of the town in Nuristan they were to go to—Kamdesh. They were given the broad mission of securing the parliamentary elections. That was it. Oles knew they needed to start getting cooperation from 1st BDE/201st Corps HQ.

Oles asked Dawson to update him on what he knew. Dawson was the 31st Kandak pay agent. Every ETT team in support of an ANA unit included a financial officer and a pay agent. Two hours ago that would have been Dawson and the major. However, as the major had maneuvered his way out of the mission, Dawson had become the titular finance officer as well as the pay agent. Only he hadn't been given the money for the mission. He informed Oles the 1st BDE Finance Officer said the money would be waiting for them in Naray. That alone seemed ridiculous to everyone. Not only was it against procedure to leave for an operation without funds, but also why would those funds be at the furthest American FOB in Kunar Province? Why couldn't they get the money now, at Asadabad? Like a pay agent was supposed to. Nothing made sense.

Oles told his NCOs to do the best they could to prepare, and each man moved off to attend to his own duties. However, Oles couldn't shake the feeling that this wasn't a normal mission. Furthermore, he couldn't help but feel that something bad was going to happen. For Oles to feel that way said a lot.

Oles was a mellow, slow-talking, unfazed kind of guy. He was the type of man who laughed often. Not a hearty laugh, but a short, quick, snicker, especially when facing something dangerous, idiotic, or ironic. Oles had already snickered several times that day. Now, preparing to head into Nuristan, Oles couldn't help but snicker again.

"When you get orders to move, usually you have a plan," he thought to himself. "We have no plan. We should have a close air support plan and a fire support plan with a battery of 105 mm howitzers. We should have a medevac plan in case we have wounded and a re-supply plan because if we have any contacts—which we're probably going to have—we are going to need ammunition and lifesavers."

Oles knew that none of those provisions existed right now, and he didn't see them materializing anytime soon. The captain inwardly wished the operation were being conducted by Marines or was at least under Marine control because, as a former Leatherneck, he felt Marine Corps doctrine prevented this kind of disorganization and operational blunders. Having served in both the Army and the Marines, Oles felt there was no comparison in the professionalism between the two. He thought the Army had a lot of catching up to do.[4]

Oles spoke with Dawson about the mission and learned they were supposed to meet one-hundred Afghan National Police (ANP) at 1500. The ANP would guide them on an undisclosed route. Dawson told his CO the ANP had threatened to leave without them and said, "I don't think they want us to go."

The ETTs hurriedly prepared, but at 1500 there were no ANP. The ETTs radioed to find out where they were and discovered the Afghan police weren't ready. Several hours later there was still no sign of the ANP, but the ANA counterparts who would accompany them on the mission showed up. They were from the Weapons Company of the 31st Kandak under the command of an ANA CPT.

With no time to spare and orders to reach Naray that day, in the late afternoon at 1830, the three Americans left Asadabad in a HMMWV heading for Naray. Longfield drove with Dawson gunning in the turret. Oles sat in the passenger side going over maps and all available intel. A column of three big Russian trucks carrying their supplies and ammunition and roughly thirty ANA soldiers of Kandak 31 followed.

Studying the maps and knowing they had zero support to date, Oles shot an email on his laptop to his Provincial Reconstruction Team Commander in Asadabad. They exchanged quick messages, and Oles learned his PRT CO was also disgusted at the lack of planning and support from higher HQ. He told Oles he had shot an email even higher and was waiting for a response. He would get Oles an answer as soon as possible.

Oles got an answer—but it wasn't what he expected. The LTC emailed Oles, telling him there was no Operations Order and he couldn't get Oles's unit any of the support he had requested. "This is not how we usually conduct business in the US Army," the LTC added, "sending Americans out into the middle of nowhere without any kind of plan." He told Oles to stand by; he would keep trying. Oles then called Coen at 2nd BDE and asked him for help, too. Coen said he would assist, and Oles felt much better knowing others were working with him on the problems.

Jalalabad

Combes was in and out of the J-Bad TOC tending to his own duties, but, as always, he tried to monitor the radio traffic when he could. He kept hearing the men on the Kamdesh mission calling for assets, calling for support, calling for orders, calling for everything. They were getting nothing! Combes had never seen or heard anything like it in his entire military service. "This is crazy!" thought Combes.

2ND BDE HQ/201st Corps; Asadabad

Coen couldn't understand why Oles and the other ETTs were having so much trouble getting cooperation and support for their mission. He checked on fire support but was told "no" because of the distance and mountainous terrain. He was given a "wait" on fixed wing CAS and a "maybe" on medevac. But the worst thing was they couldn't get an Ops order.

Coen called CFC Alpha, a colonel, and explained all the irregularities of the mission. He made clear the absurdities of not being able to get an Ops order, support, and the various other egregious aspects of the operation.

"If they can't get that stuff," said Coen, "you outta cancel the mission."

However, this reasoning did nothing but make the colonel angrier. He was already frustrated from receiving the same unanswerable questions from his own 1st BDE officers, and now he was receiving it from 2nd BDE. Coen felt the colonel had to know this was an extremely bad mission to send his men on. Both Coen's and CFC

Alpha's intel showed that HMMWVs could not make it to Kamdesh on the narrow, winding Nuristan mountain roads. For their own safety, in Afghanistan it was SOP (standard operating procedure) that all US soldiers were not to travel in anything less than an up-armored HMMWV.

Coen also knew that if Oles's battlegroup had to walk, the ETTs would lose a valuable method of commo. Blue Force tracker was the internet GPS system that allowed friendly forces to be identified on the battlefield. Only, part of that equipment was in the HMMWV. Since the narrow road prevented HMMWPs, that piece of useful technology was factored out by the mission. Not willing to give up so easily, Coen questioned the lack of intel and made a very obvious statement to his commander:

"We don't even know if we can get there."

"They will drive as far as possible, park, and walk the rest of the way."

"Sir, have you ever walked in the mountains?"

"It's a classic light infantry mission. They are going!"

Coen realized the operation was being ordered from a much higher authority. He was powerless to intervene. Although he was the team chief for the ETTs, the soldiers were not under his command and reported directly to Saber 3, a full bird colonel at 1ST BDE HQ.

A-BAD ROAD/ETT'S AND WEAPON'S CO/31ST KANDAK

Oles opened the newest email from his PRT (Provincial Reconstruction Team) CO and felt things were finally going to get done. However, the tone of the email had changed. The 1st BDE LTC had run up against a wall. CFC Alpha had told him the ETTs were going and that was that. The LTC told Oles he had to go.

Oles felt maybe his CO had gotten himself in trouble with all his questions because of the terseness of the email. Oles suspected the mission had been pushed down the Army's throat from high above. He figured it was politics. He couldn't know for sure, but with the national elections in the spotlight, Oles assumed the politicians in Washington couldn't have the UN-JEMB (United Nations Joint Election Monitoring Board) invalidate the entire parliamentary elections. Someone had to get to Kamdesh to make a show of force. Oles, Dawson, Longfield, Strate, and Midwest happened to be the unlucky five Americans chosen to accompany the ANA into remote Nuristan.

Oles then got a call from Coen. The 2nd BDE (attached) LTC had nothing but the same bad news. The mission was being pushed from higher sources.

Accepting their fate, Oles called his BDE intelligence officer and asked what they could expect. He was informed that the area of Afghanistan they were heading for was extremely remote. The coalition didn't go there. In fact, during the Russian occupation, the Russians didn't even go there. The Russian base at Naray had even been overrun by fighters from the Kamdesh area. The region was a veritable haven for the al-Qaeda and Taliban as well as Chechnians, Pakistanis, and every other type of Anti-Coalition Force. It was the type of place that attracted not just the hardcore extremists—who hailed mostly from Pakistan—but anyone who wanted to get paid for killing an American.

Bari Kowt

Midwest woke Strate up at around 1900 so he could start his shift.

"Do we have any orders yet?"

"They say we are to stay on mission."

Midwest was visibly demoralized and muttered again how this was not their mission and should be tasked to the SF.

Strate started his shift by making rounds. He circled their perimeter, visiting all the O-Ps. After making rounds he sat down to eat an MRE. It was now after dusk. He had just finished eating when gunfire erupted in the night. Strate leapt up, unslung his M-4 on the run, and raced across the compound to the O-P that had fired. Wahid was right with him. When they got to the O-P, Strate saw an ANA soldier aiming his AK out into the darkness.

"What's going on?" asked Strate. Midwest also arrived at the O-P. The ANA soldier looked terrified.

"What did you see?" asked Strate.

"I saw a mountain vampire."

Strate realized the man was serious and couldn't help but chuckle. The two Americans put on their NVGs and, with M-4s at the ready, walked into the cornfield to investigate. They walked the entire length of the field before returning to the O-P.

"There's nothing out there," assured Strate to the ANA soldiers who had gathered to see what the shooting was about. Midwest went back to his tent to rack out and Strate continued his shift. Strate called the SF to let them know they had shots fired, but that it was probably just a mountain vampire. He had to explain what he meant before he could get a chuckle out of the SF. He then gave an update on what they had been doing, finished the radio call with the SF, and headed back to the CP.

Strate spent the rest of his shift making small talk with Wahid and the ANA soldiers who weren't sleeping. He made rounds to the O-Ps and spoke to the ANA Lieutenant colonel.

"We need some supplies," stated the LTC through Wahid. The ANA colonel was in command but Strate was the pay agent; he held the unit's money—$2.5 million Afghani ($50,000 U.S. Dollars). The ANA couldn't buy anything without him.

"What supplies do you think you need?" asked Strate.

"We need soap to clean our clothes and some flashlights for guard duty."

"We can get that in the morning."

FOB Naray

The three ETTs in their HMMWV followed by the Russian trucks reached Naray at 2300 and were admitted by the SF stationed there. Their contact, Childress, was also waiting. The CPT was recently assigned to go on the mission but, like all the other orders that seemed to constantly change, Childress was suddenly told to stay behind with the ANA that remained in Naray.

Longfield drove through the Hesco walls and parked their HMMWV. The ANA pulled in beside them. Oles and his sergeants began discussing their mission with Childress and the SF. Childress was an ETT replacement staffing Naray with 1st Company, Kandak 31. Oles and Dawson knew Childress, liked him, and felt he was one of them. Oles spoke to his fellow CPT but wasn't able to learn anything positive. Oles knew he better get some help quick. Naray was their last chance—the last place they could get orders for their mission.

Oles looked around for the rest of his contingent. Two other American ETTs (Strate and Midwest) were supposed to be at Naray with the rest of the ANA.

"Where are the other two sergeants that will be accompanying us on the mission?"

"They're waiting up at Bari Kowt," replied Childress.

After discussing their situation with the SF, the ETTs prepared to bed down for the night. They would try to work out the problems in the morning.

"Beware the fury of the Legions [5]...This was the most fucked up mission I'd ever seen or even heard of. We had no Operations Order, no written orders period, nothing. They sent us out there to die. I didn't expect to come back from Nuristan."
                              Staff Sergeant James Dawson,
                              Indiana National Guard;
                              31st Kandak, 1st BDE
                              201st Corps, ANA

FOB NARAY
September 15

"Dude! This ain't a good idea."

The SF OIC was looking directly at Oles as he spoke.

"Do you remember last July? Operation Redwing? When that SEAL surveillance team was compromised in Kunar? Remember the big mission to save that last surviving SEAL? The other three died...Well, before that mission, I told those SEALs, 'This ain't a good idea.'"

Oles was harboring serious doubts about his assignment. He already had a bad feeling before he talked to the Special Forces. Now he was convinced it was a terrible idea that might get them all killed. Oles had intended to make their situation better by pumping the SF for all the intel he could get because who knew more than the Special Forces? They were professional soldiers and knew the indigenous people and the area better than any other American or coalition troops. But now, after getting this clear message from the best soldiers in Afghanistan, Oles was wondering if it would be possible to just accomplish the mission and get back alive.

"Where are the two companies of ANA infantry?" he asked. Looking around, Oles could only see the thirty men who drove up with them from Asadabad, less than a platoon.

"The rest of the ANA are waiting with the two ETTs in Bari Kowt."

"I can't believe they would send you guys in without a plan," said one of the SF operatives.

It was shortly after dawn and everyone was up, prepping for the mission. The SF knew all about the ETT operation because they had been monitoring radio communication since Strate and Midwest left for Bari Kowt on Sept 12. They were still shocked by its absurdity.

"Look, it's a bad idea," said another SF operative. "We've got imagery of that road. Come here, I'll show you."

They led Oles and Longfield into a primitive hut that was their Ops (Operations) center. Via laptop they showed them satellite pictures of the road they would be taking. It was a narrow, one-lane dirt road that snaked into the mountains. For the most part, it had sheer mountains rising on one side and a sheer drop into a river one hundred feet below on the other. The SF team sergeant just shook his head. He looked Oles square in the eye and said, "You know what…don't fuckin' go!" Then he added, "Nuristan is an R&R site for the Taliban."

Oles already knew this. The SF was giving him exactly the same intel he'd already acquired from his own BDE S-3. Nuristan was a haven for al-Qaeda, Taliban, Pakistani mercenaries, and every other ACM force in the region. It was like being in Iraq, where foreign mercenaries—what they called freedom fighters—got paid for killing Americans. Oles knew it was probably the worst area in Afghanistan for an American to go.

Bari Kowt

Strate woke Midwest at 0700. He told him what the ANA LTC had said the night before. They decided to take the ANA down to the next village to get the needed supplies. Strate, Midwest, and Wahid rode in the HMMWV while a squad of ANA followed them in two Ford Rangers. The village was about three miles down the road and right on the border of Pakistan.

The convoy drew a lot of attention as they pulled into the village. Although the locals were not used to seeing either Americans or ANA, Strate knew it was he and Midwest who were drawing most of the attention because they stood out so much. They pulled in driving a

HMMWV; the ANA drove Ford Rangers. They were white; the ANA were dark-skinned. They wore tan DCUs (desert combat uniforms); the ANA wore green BDUs.

It was surprising for Strate to see how different some of the Afghans looked in this eastern province of Afghanistan. Several of the locals had much lighter skin color. That was puzzling to Strate because they were so close to the Pakistani border and usually Pakistanis were much darker. Some of these people definitely had Caucasian skin color and features.

The ANA made their presence known. Most of them stood around and a few occasionally spoke to the locals. Others shopped for the needed supplies. Strate snapped a few pictures of the village and Midwest took one of Strate. They spent a couple of hours in town and, once they had everything they could get, they loaded their vehicles and returned to Bari Kowt.

Back at the border police station, Midwest went to check in with their CO and give him an update while Strate went to sleep. The exhausted sergeant had only been asleep for two hours when he was awakened by angry shouting. He got up to find out what was happening and saw Midwest near several ANA. The Afghan LTC was also there along with his second in command, an Afghan lieutenant (LT).

"What's goin' on?"

"The ANA don't want to go to Kamdesh," replied Midwest. "They're arguing over that."

Strate, with Wahid in tow, went over to the LTC.

"What's goin' on?"

"The soldiers don't want to go to Kamdesh."

"Well," said Strate to the LTC through Wahid, "We have orders to move to Kamdesh. We have to go, no matter what. Whether we want to or not." Strate noticed Midwest pull out his Iridium phone to call their CO at BDE. Strate could hear Midwest telling the colonel how the ANA didn't want to go to Kamdesh. Strate finished talking to the ANA LTC as Midwest got off the phone. Midwest looked dejected and Strate asked him what BDE said.

"We're to tell the ANA that we have to go." Then Midwest groaned and added, "We shouldn't be here. This is an SF mission."

Since their arrival at Bari Kowt, Strate had heard increased whining from Midwest. At first it was rare, but by the third day it was getting more frequent. When Strate first began interacting with Midwest, he tried to overlook this side of the man's personality. But lately it was getting worse.

"We shouldn't be here," Midwest complained again. "This is not our mission."

"You know what, sergeant," snapped Strate, his temper suddenly flaring, "this is your mission. As an ETT your mission is to take these men into battle."

Midwest must have realized he had no sympathy from his fellow American because he moved off to their CP. Strate returned to their tent near the HMMWV to sleep. Strate was getting fed up with the sergeant's attitude. The man was an E-7; he should know better.

Jalalabad

Combes was tending to his duties in 2nd BDE HQ when an SF major arrived at their TOC to speak to their BDE commander. Combes knew about the difficulties of the Kamdesh mission and had been trying, unsuccessfully, to help the team preparing to head there acquire assets. By now, everyone in their HQ knew it was a bad mission and would leave the soldiers on it hanging. Because it would obviously be so dangerous, everyone at Asadabad, Jalalabad, Naray, and the outlying bases was curious about the mission and listened for radio talk about it. Combes didn't need to. The talk was right in front of him. He was busy working, but not so busy that he didn't listen to what was being said.

"Hey," said the SF major to the colonel, "you guys need to be aware what you're getting into here. Those guys are going to be far out there by themselves without a whole lot of support. This isn't just going to be a drive down the road. This is going to be a more involved mission and has the potential to go bad in a hurry."

Combes's CO said he understood but the mission was ordered to proceed. He assured the SF major that they had it under control. The major didn't look convinced. He left.

Bari Kowt

Strate was asleep when he felt someone shaking him awake. It was Midwest. He actually seemed upbeat for the first time since they had left Asadabad.

"The CO said we have help coming to finish the rest of the mission."

Strate was as relieved to hear this news as Midwest was. He went to the CP just in time to take an incoming call from the SF at Naray.

"Your contingent has arrived. You need to come up here."

Strate signed off and had Wahid tell the ANA to stay in place and wait for their return in a couple hours. Then he and Midwest got in their HMMWV for the hour drive to Naray. With several ANA following behind in a Ford Ranger, they headed back to link with the others.

FOB Naray

"How do we get there?" Oles asked his Battalion Intelligence Officer (S-2) over the radio. There was no transportation allotted for the mission. The ANA infantry had their big Russian trucks, but they couldn't take them much further than Bari Kowt because of the terrain. The S-2 could give them no answers.

"Can you provide us light vehicles?

"There are none available. Nor do we have time to wait for any to be allocated. You are to acquire vehicles and if no vehicles are available, you're to use donkeys."

Oles snickered aloud at that. "Are they insane?" he thought. He had already checked the maps. Kamdesh was 75 kilometers away through some of the worst terrain imaginable.

"It will take us days to get to Kamdesh by donkey," he said. "You want us there now."

"You have your mission," said the S-2. "Carry it out."

Oles knew no one from above had put any serious thought into the operation. Although donkeys were part of theater SOP, because of the nature of the terrain and the time allotted, Oles knew animal transportation was completely unrealistic. If they had several days, it would be pseudo-plausible, but since they only had twenty-four hours to get to Nuristan, the donkey idea was senseless babble coming from higher HQ.

"Looking at the last 35 kilometers," thought Oles to himself as he scanned one of their maps, "one, if we get hit, God help us because we have no heavy weapons and no medevac. Two, it will take at least four days to walk in by donkey. We can't make it in time to secure the elections. And if we go anyway and get hit, how are we going to walk out with wounded?" Oles knew that HMMWVs wouldn't work because they were too wide. He had no idea how he was going to procure enough vehicles to complete his mission.

Dawson, the Kandak 31 pay agent, had been told someone would meet him at Naray with the money allotted for the mission. However, now he was at Naray and the money wasn't. On top of that, nobody knew anything about it. When he called back to 1st BDE to talk to the Finance Officer, he was told the money would be sent the following day. Dawson pointed out that they were leaving for Kamdesh the following day. The officer assured him the money would arrive before their departure.

The Finance Officer then explained why this irregularity had occurred. Apparently, against procedure, the money had been given to an ANA officer at BDE HQ—Colonel Jamal Nasir. The finance officer said Nasir would send an ANA LTC to Dawson with the money. In the meantime, the ETTs were to use their Title 10 money.[6]

Dawson got off the phone and seethed at the stupidity of the higher-ups. Title 10 was for emergency use only. The funds for a mission were always given to the ETTs and then doled out to the ANA and used for mission expenses. This procedure ensured that money was always available should unseen problems and operating costs arise. Money was never given to the ANA until after their service because they were constantly going AWOL. If they were paid before their service, many would just desert with their free money. Dawson felt BDE was inept and derelict of duty.

Longfield was introduced to the Afghan interpreter (Terp) who was assigned to him for the mission. Then he met the Afghan officer in command of the ANA Weapons Company they were attached to, CPT Rahim, who did not look happy to be in Naray. He didn't seem to care to meet his American counterparts, either. He moved off after a brief introduction. Looking around at the Afghan soldiers who would be accompanying them, Longfield noticed they seemed to be extremely uneasy. One thing he had learned: if the ANA were relaxed, you could relax; if the ANA looked nervous, be ready.

"What's wrong with the ANA?" he asked his Terp. "Why are they so nervous?"

"The soldiers do not want to go to Nuristan," said the Afghan in his heavily accented English. "It is very dangerous there."

"What's the captain like?"

"He do not want to go either," said the Terp.

Longfield learned that the Afghan commander hoped the mission would be cancelled. Longfield moved over to Oles and told him about the ANA's reluctance to enter a province in their own country.

"Holy shit," sighed Oles. "This isn't going to work."

Oles went into the SF CP to call back to Asadabad, again, to ask for official orders for the mission, again. He also called Coen at 2nd BDE and asked him to help get cooperation from 1st BDE. Coen said he would try.

To everyone present, it was unbelievable that 1st BDE HQ was refusing to provide written orders. Only now, the higher-ups back in Asadabad were beginning to get frustrated at their own lack of ability to get answers from above. The requests went back and forth until CFC Alpha finally said, "We don't care if you have to rent donkeys and walk. Go!"

Oles went back outside and discussed any options they might have with the SF OIC. There were none. Ultimately, everything pointed at the mission being a bad idea. What was going through Oles's mind at that moment was that the operation was going to end in disaster with their headless bodies displayed on Al Jezeera TV.

An hour after they left Bari Kowt, Strate and Midwest rolled up to Naray and were admitted inside the Hesco walls. They got out of their vehicles and Strate saw the men who would accompany him to Kamdesh.

"*Sweet!*" he said aloud, smiling broadly. He knew two of the three soldiers—Dawson and Oles. They were all Indiana Guard. Strate had trained with them and served in Bosnia with both. He had also trained with them at Fort Hood in Texas before their deployment to Afghanistan. In Bosnia, Strate and Dawson were in the same company. Oles had been the CO for a different company, but Strate knew and respected the captain and thought he was a fine officer.

Strate was relieved. Up to now it had been him and Midwest, a man Strate felt was a nice guy but in no way a soldier. Strate walked over and shook hands with Oles and Dawson. He introduced Midwest to them and met Longfield. Strate and Midwest then met the ANA battalion commander of the 31st Kandak, Rahim. The first idea that came to Strate's mind when he met the baleful looking Afghan CPT and shook his hand was, "Criminal." Strate did not trust Rahim from the moment he laid eyes on him and thought, "He's dirty."

Strate told Oles about the last four days and his inability to get any written orders from above, information Oles already knew. Oles went back into the Ops Center and got on the radio again. He wanted to have one last talk with his commanding officer back in Asadabad. If Taliban radicals were going to behead their live American bodies on television, Oles didn't want higher HQ denying everything and saying, "It was crazy ol' Captain Oles who went off on a suicide mission without orders and led his men to their deaths."

Receiving orders was important to Oles. Fearing the outcome of the mission, he needed someone to assume the risks with him so that when it ended in catastrophe, others couldn't blame him for leading the force in without orders. Oles needed his superior to say, "Seeing all these risks and contingencies, I'm telling you…go!"

Oles never told any of his superiors that he thought the operation was a bad idea. He had simply asked for SOP written orders and tried to illustrate the dangers. He had asked what resources they could provide to overcome or at least mitigate the inherent dangers of entering Nuristan. Oles continually believed his commander wanted to cancel the mission, but a political force more powerful than the military had ordered it to proceed.

"Hey, sir," he said when he got on the radio. "We will go, but I really need to hear it from you, understanding the risks."

By now the colonel must have been aggravated by the incessant radio calls because he snapped.

"Just get your ass in the truck and go!"

Longfield, Dawson, and Strate were also in the CP. They could tell the senior officer on the other end was frustrated, but all three soldiers were shocked by the informality of that final order. The SF appeared astounded. They said they had never heard of anything like this. Oles felt his commander had simply gotten tired of trying to answer questions he couldn't answer and exploded in frustration.

Longfield was rarely surprised by what happened in the Army, but this did surprise him. What disturbed him almost as much was being aware the ANA didn't even want to go to Kamdesh. They knew. They wanted no part of Nuristan and appeared terrified. Longfield was the oldest in the group, a forty-year-old sergeant and combat veteran who'd seen his share of danger. However, Longfield never had an uneasy feeling of impending doom like he had for this mission.

Dawson, although younger than Longfield by ten years and less experienced, was a similar type of NCO. He shared the same belief that you followed orders and did your duty. Sometimes you would get good duties, sometimes "shit" duties, but that was part of being in the Army. And you just had to "soldier up" and do the best job you could. To Dawson, this mission appeared to be without a doubt the "shit" duty of his Army career. Although the colonel had been the one they heard over the radio, Dawson felt the order had to have come from even higher. He blamed the General, the colonel's commanding officer.

Oles and his sergeants continued to discuss the situation with the SF. They kept telling Oles the mission was a bad idea, using words like "crazy", "fucked up", and "suicidal". To a man the SF were shaking their heads. Then one of them said, "That road is impassable. Have another look, I'll show you."

Using imagery from predator aircraft, the SF showed the ETTs how the road was washed out where the river had recently overflowed in half a dozen places. The SF referred to it as the Nuristan Road.[7]

"We wouldn't go there," warned an SF NCO to Longfield, "You guys shouldn't go."

"We don't wanna go, but we don't have an option. We've been ordered to go."

The SF OIC gave Oles the same rundown about the known enemy in their area that they had showed Strate four days prior. They told him about everything the soldiers might possibly run up against. The guardsmen were given a list of the local players—mostly bad guys. Because the province of Nuristan and the village of Kamdesh were right along the Pakistani border, there were a lot of them. A couple of towns were heavily targeted and constantly watched for al-Qaeda. Mandagal appeared to be the worst.

The guardsmen listened carefully to everything the SF said. The role of the ETTs working with the indigenous military was originally a SF mission, but there were simply not enough SF to work with so many native soldiers. Therefore, the Guard had to step in to help and, in Afghanistan, they provided most of the manpower.

Oles was surprised when the SF OIC called his own superior to try to get their mission scrubbed. He overheard the conversation.

"We don't even send SF in there," said the OIC. "Do you really think it's wise to send National Guard in there with ANA?"

Oles felt better. The SF carried clout. Surely higher HQ would listen to them. An answer came back soon enough. Except, again, it wasn't the answer they had expected. The SF was told not to interfere with the mission. More than anything else, this message convinced Oles that the orders came from an authority higher than the Army.

Oles swapped their HMMWV for Childress's Ford Ranger and the ETTs transferred all their ammunition and supplies to the pick-up. Strate and Midwest also exchanged their HMMWV for a SF Ford Ranger. The SF feared what was going to happen, so they loaded their fellow Americans with extra ammo, grenades, and CLSs. The combat lifesaver was the equivalent of a first-aid kit capable of treating two severely wounded soldiers. Everyone was CLS qualified but they worried about re-supply and refills.

Oles and his men shook hands with the SF and Childress and headed for their vehicles.

"Hang tough," said one operative. The SF OIC gave a final warning and said, "Hey, past Bari Kowt, that's as far as we can go. We can't help you."

Oles understood. A line had been drawn and the SF couldn't cross it.

The convoy left the FOB gates at Naray and drove to Bari Kowt, an hour to the north. The column made good time and reached the village without incident.

Oles looked around at the meager troops in Bari Kowt and asked, "What happened to the two companies of infantry we're supposed to have?"

It was then Oles got another surprise. He had been told he would have two companies under his command. That sounded good on paper as an ANA company had 110 men. However, Oles didn't allot for so much "Afghan math". He wasn't naïve enough to think he'd have the standard force of two companies, 220 heavily-armed soldiers—a sizeable force—but he did not think there would be fewer than 100 men. When he learned the size of the force he was leading into Nuristan included only sixty-seven men—less than two platoons of infantry—he groaned in frustration.

The ANA officers explained through Oles's Terp that sick calls and almost 140 AWOLs had decimated the ranks of both ANA Companies. Oles was a positive person by nature, but looking around at the two platoons he would lead into Nuristan, he thought, "This keeps going from bad to worse."

Oles also saw there would be friction within the ANA command structure in his battlegroup. His two ANA Companies were from two different Weapons Companies in two separate battalions. One was part of Kandak 31 and the other was part of the Kandak 34. The CO of the 34th Kandak was a LTC and battalion commander. He was in overall command of the ANA battlegroup. The CO of the company from the 31st Kandak was Rahim. The two ANA officers took an immediately dislike to each other the moment their two units joined in Bari Kowt. Oles, Dawson, and Longfield were with Kandak 31, and Strate and Midwest were with the 34th.

SSG Scott Strate with ANA troops in a village near Bari Kowt, Afghanistan

Photo taken near Bari Kowt

September 14, Wednesday

Tried to meet the flight at 0800 to put Longfield on — then it would come back and we'd helo in, but the helo never came. We've been told the road is washed out but at 1500 we're to meet 100 ANP who'll guide us over the secret road. They called & said we're leaving with or without the US. I don't think they want us to go. At 1500 there were no police and they weren't ready to go. The plan was to go by truck then walk 25K into Kamdesh. We left at 1830 and got to Nariah around 1100.

September 15, Thursday

New Plan — take vehicles in then rent donkeys. We have no Op order or Risk Assessment so we asked Coen to sign off on it and he took it higher. We were told by Gen Perry m'n': "Get your ass on the truck and go." There's supposed to be 150+ ACM and we're in Ford Rangers, travelling a narrow washed out road. Also we're supposed to spend our title 10 on them. It's for emergencies, not a lack of planning! So some genius is sending 25KB with an ANA officer, brilliant! Now they'll skim and we'll still hear "must have MRE, Peps;". Whatever, Nasir went to Abad for his Cut and might come back. This goes against a lot of rules the Army has & we're getting hung out to dry.

James Dawson's Journal entries from September 14 and 15

"I believe that the order to execute came from the highest levels. Having the UN invalidate the entire parliamentary elections would have set the country back even further. But I don't know the answer. Once the order came down we didn't dither, we executed."

Captain Marc Oles,
Indiana National Guard
Team Chief, 31st Kandak
1st BDE, 201st Corps, ANA

INSERTION
September 16

Everyone was up early trying to acquire the resources they had been unable to obtain for the last few days. It was then Oles received his first good news. His Terp informed him the ANA had rounded up fifteen Toyota Hilux pickup trucks[8]. Oles was amazed they had been able to come up with the vehicles so quickly. Finally, something was working in their favor.

"Where did you get them," he asked his Terp.

"From civilians."

"They just gave them to you?"

"No, they were requisition."

Pause.

"How?"

The interpreter explained that the civilians were approached to give up their trucks for the government and a worthy cause.

"And they said, 'yes'?" Oles was extremely surprised that so many people would acquiesce to losing their vehicles.

"No, they refuse."

"…So how did you get them?"

"The soldiers say, 'Would you like to help out your country and rent out your truck?' The person say, 'No.' Then the soldier say, 'Well, I have gun.'"

"You can't do that," groaned Oles, knowing it was already done. "We need to find those civilians and give them receipts for their vehicles."

Oles shook his head in frustration. He knew more than anything how important it was to keep the local population believing in the integrity of the new government and its US and coalition allies. Without that belief, they would appear no different than the Taliban. And now the ANA had simply carjacked fifteen vehicles from civilians.

In fact, the feelings of civilians was a massive, growing problem. The average Afghan believed the government to be more corrupt than the Taliban.[9] Using their Terps, the Americans attempted to find all the civilians from whom the trucks were requisitioned in order to give them receipts for the use of their trucks. Oles found to his greater surprise they didn't have to look far to find many of those civilians. Worried they would never see their vehicles again, several owners decided to accompany the week-long mission as rented drivers. The civilians were temporarily "assigned" to the mission.

The ANA and ETTs promised to pay for each day the vehicle was used, take care of the vehicle during its rental, and assured the Afghans that if something happened to the trucks, the government of Afghanistan (basically the US) would reimburse them. Despite these assurances, none of the civilians looked happy about the requisition of their vehicles, especially those accompanying the mission, even though they would also get paid a daily rate as a driver. The ETTs felt the ANA didn't appear to care one way or the other whether the civilians ever saw their vehicles again.

They worried even more about another potentially-incapacitating problem. Dawson's money had still not arrived. Oles, Longfield, and Dawson had only the Title 10 money for the mission. Dawson had been told the cash would be waiting at Naray. At Naray he was told it would be brought to them at Bari Kowt. Now he was at Bari Kowt—and the money wasn't.

Oles asked Strate and Midwest if they had been given the money. Strate said no. He had only been allotted the money for Kandak 34, not Dawson's Kandak 31. Strate knew nothing about the money for Kandak 31.

Calling back to 1st BDE HQ, Oles again asked about the money and was told it should have arrived already. The BDE finance officer assured him the money allotted for the mission would soon arrive with an Afghan LTC.

When the LTC arrived, Dawson went over to him to procure the $2,000,000 Afghani. The ANA LTC was angry when he learned he was to give the money to Dawson, which made the Americans wonder who he thought he was going to give it to. They assumed he must have intended to give it to Rahim, which probably meant the LTC could take his cut and nobody would know the difference. At least, that was what made sense to them to account for his irrational anger at having to do what he was sent to do because now he'd have to turn it all over.

Longfield explained the ANA were always paid after the operation or after their month of service, as this officer well knew. It didn't help. The Afghan officer worked himself into a rage. He refused to hand over the money. Had Longfield or Dawson been an American lieutenant colonel or even a major, Longfield felt the Afghan officer might not have become so irate. But because they were NCOs, he was adamant; it was his money.

So began an hour-long confrontation with many radio calls back to both ANA headquarters and American headquarters at Phoenix. More and more time was being wasted. The standoff finally ended with the seething ANA officer returning $1,000,000 Afghani to Dawson.

"Where's the other million?"

Another hours-worth of radio calls ensued, with Longfield and Dawson trying to find out what happened to the remaining $1,000,000 Afghani. It was then the ETTs learned about the money trail. An American colonel had wanted to show his trust and comradeship toward his ANA counterpart, an Afghan general. He had simply handed over the $2,000,000 Afghani for the mission. The ANA general had given it to his subordinate, Colonel Jamall Nasir, their ANA battalion commander, who gave it to the LTC. Exactly how much of the money was pocketed by any of the three was not known, but, finally, Longfield was told by 1st BDE HQ to continue the mission with only the $1,000,000 Afghani and not to ask any more questions.

In mounting frustration, Longfield went to tell Oles this latest news. Longfield had been in Afghanistan before and had seen how corruption inside the ANA was dismantling US efforts from within. The missing money was now lining the pockets of at least one ANA officer and maybe four more people, including Rahim, whom the LTC met the moment he arrived. It made Longfield sick but there was nothing he could do. Oles could do nothing, either, except continue the mission.

With no Ops Order and no direction from above other than "Go", Oles made his own mission orders. There was only one road to Kamdesh. The last site where they could expect any local help was at Gowerdash where there was an ANP (Afghan National Police) Station. Beyond that, the Nuristan Road snaked along a mountain river from Gowerdash to Kamdesh and then into Pakistan. They had to travel on that road because there was no other way. If they got hit and it got ugly, their only option was to escape and evade back down the river to the border police at Gowardesh.

Throughout the mission, they would try to maintain communication with BDE and the SF. This was some comfort because Oles figured if they had trouble, maybe the SF could send help via some of their Afghan lackeys. Out on the border the SF had its own local Afghan forces. There was also possible help from the Afghan Police and the ASF (Afghan Security Forces). The CIA even had forces in the area: CTPTs (Counter Terrorism Pursuit Teams), which were the CIA's own secret Afghan army. There were so many little private armies, all armed to the teeth, aside from the regional warlords with their own militia factions (most of which did not wear uniforms) that the entire countryside bristled with weapons and troops.

As they prepared to roll out, Oles made a final effort to acquire air support. After several attempts, he quickly realized there was no way they were going to get air-dropped into Nuristan. He was also unable to get an affirmative answer about receiving close air support, once there. The Coalition Air Force was worried about surface to air missiles, and the ANA Air Force flat out refused to fly into Nuristan. Oles got off the radio. Aviation was not an option.

Oles discovered the SF was still monitoring all their radio transmissions because they called him in astonishment. They were almost laughing at these latest tales of woe—the money issues and the hundred plus Afghan AWOLs. They said again that they'd never seen or heard of anything like it.

Four of the Americans were extremely reluctant to continue with the mission. The fifth man was absolutely "nervous-in-the-service". That was Midwest, the NCO from the breadbasket region of the U.S. He wanted no part of this mission and offered several ideas to Oles including the suggestion they not go but radio back that they did. Oles snickered and shook his head. "We've been ordered in. We're going."

The die was cast. It was time to execute. With bungee cord and hundred-mile-an-hour tape, Oles rigged the SAT COM (Satellite Communication) radio to the back of his truck cab and boarded his vehicle. Communications would be intermittent because of the mountains, but it was the best they could do. Besides his SAT COM, they also had Strate and Midwest's Iridium phone and two Thuraya phones. Strate's TAC SAT radio remained with the HMMWV in Naray.

The battlegroup rolled out with a grand total of 67 soldiers, less than two platoons, and a dozen civilian drivers. The other ETTs were painfully aware it was the AWOLs who made up over 90 % of the ANA absentees. With 25 supply- and munitions-laden pickup trucks, verbal orders, and a pressing time frame, the convoy rolled out of Bari Kowt heading into Nuristan.

Almost immediately the road became dangerously narrow. Their pace slowed to a crawl. The region was mountainous and unforgiving and it only promised to get worse. To Oles the road looked like ambush lane. And to make matters worse, their force was driving in unarmored pickup trucks. Throughout his time in Afghanistan, Oles had always been ordered to have his men drive in up-armored HMMWVs. Yet here they were, on the most dangerous mission he'd ever seen, driving in unarmored pickup trucks, the only vehicles available.

It was early evening, just after dusk. The traveling was slow because it was pitch dark. The single dirt lane was very hazardous and snaked into the mountains. Because they were traveling at night, the vehicles had to use their lights. The road itself was more dangerous than an ACM or Taliban ambush, so the battlegroup couldn't chance moving in the dark without them.

There was a sheer rock face rising several hundred feet on one side and a sheer drop one hundred feet down into freezing class-three rapids on the other. The water was ice-cold in the river. Oles and his men knew that because on three occasions they had to descend and ford the river where the road wound through it.

"This is so fucked up," thought Oles. "One route in; one route out. They can hit us whenever and wherever they want."

Longfield had similar thoughts. He knew if they got hit, there was not even a spot along the narrow road where a helicopter could get in to evacuate their wounded.

Oles had rigged the lead vehicle with a big searchlight he had brought from Indiana while on leave. The light would scan the ridges above for any sign of movement. Unfortunately, Oles suspected if they got ambushed, the light would be the first thing the enemy shot out.

The convoy moved further away from Bari Kowt and snaked into a valley where they would roll up to the Saw Bridge at Gowardesh and cross into Nuristan. According to the map they were only one bend in the road away from the Saw Bridge. At 2100 they rounded a spur in the mountain and found themselves entering a battle.

The Province of Nuristan. Kamdesh is in the upper right near the Pakistani boarder.

"In Afghanistan, everybody's got a cell phone - they are illiterate, they ride on donkeys, and they wipe their ass with rocks, but everyone's got a cell phone. We weren't even in Nuristan yet and the ACM was calling ahead, telling their friends we were coming,"

SFC Class Don Longfield,
Oklahoma National Guard
31st Kandak 1st BDE, 201st Corps

GOWARDESH
September 16-17

"Holy shit!" said Oles as he took in the scene. They rounded a rocky bend that led to the Saw Bridge at Gowardesh, and the noise was as shocking as the sight. In the darkness ahead tracers and RPGs (Rocket Propelled Grenades) could be seen flying back and forth across the river. The report of automatic weapons and small arms fire was deafening. Explosions erupted on both sides of the valley, lighting up the night for just an instant before disappearing. Oles's convoy had rolled into a battle. Because of the orange color of the tracer fire, Oles and Longfield could tell the ANP at Gowardesh were firing PKM machineguns. Both sides were hammering away at each other with AKs, too, as was evident by the ubiquitous green tracers, and the far side was launching RPGs. Their explosions detonated in brilliant yellow, orange, and red eruptions.

The convoy drove right up to the fight. Oles and his Terp got out of the vehicle and moved forward to try to figure out what was going on. All Oles could make out initially was that a bunch of people were shooting at each other. Behind him, the ANA quickly dismounted their vehicles and began firing across the river up at the ridges.

"CONSERVE YOUR AMMUNITION!" shouted Oles, "GET BACK IN YOUR TRUCKS!" It was too late; the ANA were setting up and blasting away.

"CEASE FIRE! GET BACK IN THE TRUCKS! CONSERVE AMMUNITION!" bellowed Oles. Longfield, Dawson, and Strate were also shouting at the ANA. The three American NCOs were trying to get their Terps to instruct the ANA officers to have their men maintain fire discipline and get back into their vehicles.

Oles noticed a shadow approaching from ahead. He and his Terp moved up to meet it in the darkness. It was a border policeman. Thankfully, the SF had informed him they were coming. The Afghan told Oles via Terp that they were engaging an unknown enemy force, probably a militia from one of the local warlords.

Oles's orders were to get to Kamdesh. All they were doing now was wasting their limited ammunition. Figuring they couldn't influence the fight with the enemy across the river, Oles had his Terp tell the Afghan police official they were going to keep moving. He asked the police to keep the opposing force suppressed with covering fire. By now, under the incessant bellowing orders of Oles, Strate and Dawson, the ANA were slowly pulling out of the fight and reluctantly re-boarding their vehicles. Oles moved back to the column and had his Terp order the lead truck to keep moving. The two leaped on their vehicle and the convoy started forward again.

FOB NARAY

The SF was monitoring Oles's convoy via predator aircraft. They knew the Guardsmen weren't even in Nuristan yet, but they had already made contact with the enemy. They called higher HQ and alerted them of this first contact.

2/3 MARINES HQ; JALALABAD

Although 2nd BDE was Army, Coen and the rest of the 2nd BDE staff were actually in Task Force Devil's (2/3 Marines) area of operation (AO), so they shared the Marines' command center. Coen was very impressed by the Marines and their professionalism. He had seen it time and again and grudgingly admitted the Army could learn a lot from the Marines. Coen thought inwardly that if his ETTs had been working with the Marines, they wouldn't be in their present situation.

The 2/3 Marines command center had flat screen TVs, intel from unmanned aircraft, and everything Coen called the "Gee-Whiz" stuff. Coen listened as the first contact was reported. Sipper Net was the secure communications network the Army used to talk back and forth via satellite. It was portable and could be carried on a man's body. That was how everyone in the CP knew what was going on. Coen and the others were listening intently for any communications between Oles and 1st BDE.

THE SAW BRIDGE

Tracer fire kicked up around them and stabbed by as the lead vehicles moved across the Bridge. The entire convoy followed. From the backs of their trucks many of the ANA were still firing. A few were just unloading rounds on full automatic.

    Normally, both Coalition and ANA units drove at night in blackout. However, the Nuristan Road was far too dangerous for the battlegroup to turn their lights off, even during a battle. If a driver made one mistake on that road, everyone in his vehicle could die. The soldiers would rather risk enemy fire than drive off a cliff into the freezing river below. Some of the ANA kept firing as the trucks slowly passed the bridge, but the enemy had pulled back.

    Oles had watched the enemy fire lessen considerably, then disappear altogether and wondered if their presence had something to do with it. He figured the enemy saw all these reinforcements approaching and thought they were a QRF (Quick Reaction Force). Whoever that opposing force was, they couldn't know it was simply an accident that this long column of twenty-five vehicles had arrived. And, the ANA troops had jumped off the trucks firing from the hip. From their tracers and RPG trails, a lot of rushing figures could be seen entering the battle. Oles felt the enemy must have thought a significant, well-armed QRF had arrived.

    Longfield thought the same thing and knew several phone calls were now being made, alerting anyone who might be interested in knowing ANA troops were entering Nuristan from Gowardesh. Longfield was amazed so many people in Afghanistan couldn't read and didn't use toilet paper, yet they had cell phones.

    The column moved past the bridge and headed north on the west bank. As they kept moving, the shooting was soon far behind them. All that could be heard were the engines of fifteen Toyota pickup trucks and ten Ford Rangers. Oles and the others were painfully aware the enemy now could attack them whenever and wherever they wanted. As the SF had made so poignantly clear to them, there was only one road in and one road out, and they had already been discovered.

    The convoy continued snaking along the Nuristan Road moving at a slow crawl. They averaged barely six mph and sometimes moved even slower as the road worsened. The ANA had no night vision and none of the vehicles had blackout capabilities, so the convoy continued with lights from twenty-five trucks shining like beacons in the night. Even with the headlights it was difficult for the soldiers to see well. Most of the trucks were UK (United Kingdom) style with the steering wheel on the right. The passenger side occupant had to keep his head out the left side window while shining a flashlight down at the left front tire to warn the driver if he was getting too close to the cliff's edge. Thankfully, there was a full moon. This helped the drivers immensely.

    Longfield drove one of the Ford Rangers. Oles and Dawson rode in the back. Strate and Midwest rode in the back of a pickup directly in front of them. Longfield knew the area they were traveling in was ripe for ambush but there was nothing he could do about it. He'd been on the receiving end of an ambush two years earlier on October 12, 2003, during his first tour in Afghanistan. That night, his CO had been shot six times in a firefight near a derelict Russian tank park the local populas called The Bone Yard. Then it had taken an hour for the QRF to arrive. Now, there was no QRF, period! They were completely on their own.

    Longfield initially joined the Ohio Army National Guard in 1982 while still in high school as a radio mechanic. He went Active Duty Army in 1985 and changed jobs to Radio Teletype Operator. Longfield stayed on active duty for almost eight years during which he was stationed at Fort Hood, Texas, Schwaebisch Gmuend, Germany, and Fort Knox, Kentucky. He got married in 1988 while transferring from Fort Hood to Germany. His daughter was born in Germany just before the start of Desert Storm. Upon returning to the United States, Longfield joined the Oklahoma Army National Guard in 1993. This was a result of the Army's downsizing after the first Gulf War. He became Infantry in 1995. He had been in several different units and had deployed to Bosnia as well as Afghanistan prior to this deployment. However, he felt his present situation was the worst he'd ever been in.

Longfield was driving more carefully than he'd ever done before. It was very disconcerting to make each of the many turns. He kept waiting for one of the vehicles ahead to teeter and fall off the cliff into the river below. The closer they got to Kamdesh, the worse the road became. Longfield thought about what would happen in the event of an attack or a breakdown. He was prepared to load all the Americans onto one truck and push any derelict vehicle(s) into the river to clear the road.

The men manning the floodlight in the back of the lead pickup shot its beam along the mountain ridges. They were looking for signs of movement or anything that might appear suspicious. At about 2200, several kilometers east of Kamdesh proper, the spotlight flashed on silhouettes above and across the river. Oles knew the Taliban or ACM usually kept themselves on the opposite side of the river to prevent any opposing force from closing with them. That was why there were rarely decisive engagements to date in Afghanistan. No force could close on an opposing force. In this case, if that was their intention, the ANA with their American ETTs would have to go ten kilometers out of their way to find a place to cross the river—if they had the sufficient strength to engage.

When the light silhouetted the figures on the opposite high ridge, the lead vehicles stopped. This forced the rest of the column to halt. Oles jumped down from his truck and moved forward to see what the hold-up was. He rounded a curve along the mountain road and saw the spotlight pinned on several men on the distant cliff.

By now Dawson had also moved forward and Strate had jumped down from his own truck. Longfield, as a driver, had not gotten out of the Ranger.

"Why the fuck did we stop?" asked Longfield to no one in particular. Tired of waiting, he too got out of the truck. The ANA were looking and pointing toward the ridges above and across the river.

"Why did we stop?" Longfield asked his Terp. He had lost sight of Oles or Dawson. They had moved up to the lead vehicles and disappeared around a bend in the road. Longfield's Terp reiterated the question to several ANA soldiers nearby. An excited reply came from several men, and the Terp said, "They saw movement across the river."

Oles was up front watching the silhouettes on the far ridge. One of the Terps ahead shouted across the river but Oles didn't understand what he said. Suddenly there were tracers flying everywhere. Oles didn't know who started the shooting, but green tracers from AKs and orange tracers from PKM machineguns were blasting back and forth across the river. Everyone was scrambling for cover. Oles could tell they were taking and giving a lot of fire.

He ran to get on his radio to report this second contact. When he got to the truck, however, to his dismay he found the radio was out. The bouncing around on the uneven roads had damaged it. Oles couldn't raise anyone.

"Shit." he said in frustration. "If we take wounded, we can't even call for medevac." He realized it was a moot point anyway. There was nowhere for medevac to land.

FOB NARAY

The SF had been monitoring the Guardsmen and their ANA counterparts via Predator Aircraft since they left Naray. They watched this second contact erupt almost directly between Gowardesh and Kamdesh. The SF was convinced the five Americans accompanying the ANA battlegroup into Nuristan were dead men. The convoy had already had two contacts and they hadn't even reached Kamdesh yet. The SF immediately called in the contact, so within moments of the firefight (unbeknown to the guardsmen), 1st BDE headquarters knew of it. The SF thought they were watching another Operation Redwing. Only this time, they suspected there wouldn't be as much effort put into a rescue—because as far the government or the press was concerned, five National Guardsmen wouldn't rate anywhere near four Navy SEALs. And Oles and his ETTs were in Nuristan, not Kunar.[10]

2/3 MARINES HQ; ASADABAD

Coen, too, sat and watched the second contact brewing via satellite. It would have felt surreal for him, except he knew the soldiers being shot at. He knew it was very real for them and he was extremely frustrated. CFC Alpha (outside Kabul) and Blackhorse (201st Corps) had taken over and gone right past the normal command chains, past BDE, and there was nothing anyone could do about it. Now five ETTs were in their second contact in less than two hours. Coen could only pray they would live through it.

Jalalabad

Combes and the brigade staffers in the J-Bad TOC couldn't help but hear the radio traffic coming from Naray and Asadabad back to Kabul about this second firefight. The ETTs were involved in another contact and they weren't even in Kamdesh yet. Combes wanted to leap up and assemble a QRF—but there was no QRF available. He wanted to get in a truck himself and go with a handful of ETTs, but even if he could get permission, which he couldn't, it would take hours to reach Oles's men. All he could do was listen in frustration for radio traffic on the command net.

NURISTAN ROAD

Longfield watched the ANA let go with everything they had. He wondered if they were even in contact. With the ANA, he never knew. When one of them fired, they all fired. And they didn't just fire one round, either. They had to let go with everything. In the middle of the twenty-five-vehicle column, Longfield watched PKMs blaze away and RPG trails fly across the river.

"What is going on?" he thought. "Are we in contact or is this just the ANA firing at nothing?" Longfield stayed at his vehicle, standing in the open door. He was trying to get a look around but at the same time be able to operate the vehicle and/or the radio. He knew the most important thing was to keep moving. They couldn't just stay where they were, and he wondered if anyone else realized this as well. Suddenly, an invisible force blew him from the door of his vehicle. Simultaneously, a tremendous heat burned him and knocked him to the ground amid a swirling vacuum of dust. Longfield was deaf from the explosion but managed to stay conscious.

"Oh, shit," he said to himself. "We're taking fuckin' rockets." Longfield rolled and got up, thinking, "Okay, here we fuckin' go. We made contact." But as Longfield stood, he saw an ANA soldier standing in front of him holding a RPG launcher. The soldier had fired without checking to see if anyone was behind him. Longfield knew if he'd been any closer, he'd be dead.

Dawson was trying to get the ANA shooters to coordinate their fire. They were spraying rounds all over the place, and many of them didn't appear to be aiming at the few muzzle-flashes across the river. Dawson returned fire at a flash, hoping the ANA would see his repeated tracer strikes in the same area, but it didn't work. Then he wondered if it was even a muzzle flash he had seen. So many bullets were ricocheting off the rocks on the far side of the valley it might have been a ricochet.

Occasionally a round would plink against the sides of their trucks, but most of the incoming was inaccurate. The hand-full of shooters (whether Taliban, ACM, or rogue) were just as bad as the ANA where marksmanship was concerned.

Strate was shouting for the ANA to get organized. They were blasting all over the place. Strate saw a muzzle flash across the river and cracked off several rounds at it from his M-4.

Oles knew they were not in a good position. The enemy was above and firing down on them. Their convoy was pinned on a one-lane road with nowhere to maneuver. Oles was anxious the enemy was going to use RPGs to blow up the lead vehicle and trap them. That's what anyone with tactical sense would do because it would halt the entire convoy until they could push the destroyed vehicle into the river. Turning around was not an option.

Oles knew the only thing they could do was to keep moving. But they couldn't all go. They needed to leave an element in contact to suppress the enemy.

He ordered his Terp to have the ANA LTC leave an element in contact while the rest of the convoy continued on. He instructed the Terp to tell them to break contact and leap on the last two vehicles as they passed. The Terp relayed the order to the LTC. The equivalent of a squad continued firing while everyone else was ordered back in their trucks by screaming, shouting ANA officers, Terps, and Americans.

Oles muttered in frustration at the lack of discipline of the ANA soldiers. Some obeyed, albeit reluctantly; others kept firing as officers screamed at them. Oles moved down the line of vehicles bellowing for everyone to keep moving. Unbelievably, his big searchlight hadn't been hit yet. The enemy either wasn't shooting at it or they were very bad shots. Wherever it shined, the shooting stopped and the shadows above faded back into the cliffs to avoid being silhouetted.

Oles got the lead trucks going and was moving back along the column when he saw a wounded man. It was the stocky American sergeant from the Midwest who suggested they not go on the mission but report they did.

"Oh, no!" thought Oles. "We've already got an American wounded. If we ever make radio contact, where the hell can we land a medevac?" Then he thought, "…if they'll even come." He ran over to check the extent of Midwest's wounds and found, to his surprise, the NCO wasn't even hit. He was curled up, taking cover.

"GET BACK TO YOUR SECTION AND GET YOUR MEN IN THEIR VEHICLES!" shouted Oles angrily. "WE HAVE TO KEEP MOVING! WE CAN'T GET TIED UP FIRING AND WASTING AMMUNITION ON THIS ROAD!" The NCO looked like he was terrified, but he got up and quickly jumped into the back of his truck without saying a word to any of the ANA under his command. The truck was following the lead vehicles. Meanwhile, the element in contact continued returning fire from the nearby rocks.

Oles kept moving down the line shouting for the ANA to board their trucks and keep moving. He saw Dawson and Strate directing the ANA, telling them to get into their vehicles. With the help of their Terps, they were able to get the entire convoy moving again. They all jumped into passing trucks or ran to catch up to their original vehicle. As the last two pickups passed, the squad in contact leapt aboard. The shooting didn't end there, though. The unit in contact continued firing at the cliffs until the last vehicle snaked out of sight some 500 meters toward Kamdesh.

"Holy shit!" thought Oles as they moved deeper into Nuristan. "We haven't even reached Kamdesh and we've already had two contacts. This is bad." And worse, Oles hadn't seen even one site suitable for landing a helicopter. "If we need a medevac, which we probably are going to need, we have to find a spot where we can land a bird the minute we reach Kamdesh."

"This is fucked," thought Longfield as drove with his head out the window, looking down at the road. He couldn't even watch for the enemy on the cliffs above because he had to keep his eyes on the road. The greater danger was still driving off the cliff. Angrily, he thought about their situation. "First, we can't get any air support for this mission before we leave. Second, none of the ANA even want to come here and our own SF tells us not to. Third, we have two contacts before we even get to Kamdesh and I don't see us getting an ammo re-supply. Worst of all is this road. Fuck, this is not a good place to be and we're not even there yet. And worse, there is only one way in and the fuckin' ACM know we're here."

Dawson was cynical by nature. Certain events made him more so. He shook his head at the overwhelming response of the ANA. Dawson didn't have any problem with the ANA trying to destroy their enemy, it made the enemy shooters fade back into the cliffs, if there were any. It was their lack of discipline and wild shooting in all directions that exasperated him. Dawson saw ANA letting go on full automatic and launching RPGs where there weren't even muzzle-flashes. They had blown up rocks and shot up cliffs because they thought they saw something. He was even less impressed with the ACM or Taliban marksmanship. Whoever had been firing at them hadn't been trying very hard. Dawson couldn't see how anyone could miss a column of twenty-five vehicles with lights beaming.

Oles was aware that all but one of his sergeants had done their job. Strate, Dawson, and Longfield had done well. They had all worked hard at keeping the element together and the drivers moving. Dawson had been directing the ANA fire even though most of the ANA were shooting at the wrong spot. Oles thought of all the wasted ammunition at both the Saw Bridge and now this second contact.

"Well, fuck," he said to himself. "Maybe at least it scared somebody." The only man whose performance was not up to standard was Midwest. He'd been taking cover in a ditch during the firefight. He only got out from defilade to board his truck to get out of there.

The convoy continued on to Kamdesh, expecting the worst. It was only 75 kilometers from FOB Naray, but they had been traveling at six mph. They finally reached the village at 2300 without further incident. When they drove into Kamdesh, an Afghan police officer walked up to talk to the soldiers in the lead vehicle. They spoke briefly and the vehicles kept moving. The Afghan policeman peered into each vehicle as it passed. When Longfield's Ford Ranger pulled abreast the police officer, Longfield braked to talk to him. The Afghan policeman saw Oles in the back of the truck and broke into a wide, toothless grin.

"Welcum-tu-Nuristan," he beamed in a thick accent. "You Americans will die."

Oles just looked at the policeman, who held his Cheshire grin. Oles thought the man's big, "stupid-looking", toothless smile in itself was scary, let alone his greeting.

Longfield had his window down and was looking at the Afghan policeman. He heard the greeting and thought to himself, "Well…I'm kind of glad I haven't died yet."

"You American's shud not be here," the man continued, still smiling. "You are going-t-get killed." Oles noticed stirring in the village. The locals were getting up and coming over to find out what was going on. They wanted to see who was in these approaching vehicles.

The policeman told Oles's Terp where he could find the village elders, and the convoy continued on. Longfield wondered if they would live through the next twenty-four hours. He believed a U.S. presence in larger numbers would have been safer (or at least comforting), but with only five Americans they would be targets. There were bounties on the heads of US soldiers. There were bounties on ANA officers and Terps as well, but they weren't worth as much as a Muslim got for killing an American. The latest figure was $1,000 US for proof of a dead American. A camera or cell phone camera snapshot standing over that dead American was enough proof.

Looking at some of the Nuristan locals, Longfield was pretty sure there were ACM in the crowd. If so, they were obviously gathering intelligence because Longfield could see several people talking on their cell phones. He assumed they were reporting the exact number of vehicles and troops (both ANA and American) now driving into Kamdesh.

Longfield drove to a small stone building where an Afghan policeman was waving for them to stop. Several men came out and Oles dismounted his vehicle. The ANA LTC walked up as did the ANA CPT. Introductions were made and Oles's group met the leader of the local security force. They were the closest thing to friends the Americans were going to have. Oles felt this security force was nothing more than the local warlord and his cronies, and they didn't look very happy to see them. After a brief discussion it was decided the ANA convoy (and American ETTs) should push up the road another 20 kilometers toward Mandagal. There they would rent several small buildings and make their bivouac. This made Oles very uneasy. Mandagal was the area known for being especially rife with bad guys— Taliban, al-Qaeda, ACM, and foreign mercenaries. It was even closer to the Pakistani border than Kamdesh.

The impromptu meeting ended and the Americans and their ANA comrades got back in their vehicles. They continued their slow crawl down the Nuristan Road. As the convoy snaked past Kamdesh toward Mandagal, Oles continued to look for a HLZ (Helicopter Landing Zone). He wanted a site suitable for landing a medevac helicopter. Dawson, Strate, and Longfield were doing the same thing. They passed one site that looked good, so Oles had his Terp stop and ask one of the local authorities about using it. The reply was that last year an American helicopter had tried to land on the site, but on its way down, a cow had run in terror from the helicopter and exploded when it detonated a land mine. That cow's death probably saved an American helicopter and its crew. Oles didn't see anything to cause him to believe the field had been cleared of mines. Later he would have it checked, but for now he and the others kept moving toward Mandagal and looking for a usable landing site.

"They knew right where we were. They could choose when and where to hit us and all we could do was wait for them to do it."

Captain Marc Oles

KAMDESH
September 17

"This is the *Deliverance* of Afghanistan," thought Longfield. He was referring to the infamous Burt Reynolds movie. The sergeant mentioned this to his Terp and asked why Kamdesh and the surrounding area seemed so different from anyplace else in Afghanistan. Longfield was surprised his Terp seemed so nervous. He obviously didn't like what he was seeing, but the American sergeant didn't know what that meant. The Terp explained to him that the people of Nuristan were not considered to be true Afghans or true Muslims. He told Longfield that until the turn of the century, they worshipped the old gods. They had converted to Islam, but they were still not considered true Muslims by their fellow Afghans because they still incorporated some of their old beliefs into their version of the Muslim faith.

It reminded Longfield of what he had read about how the Haitians had incorporated some of their old Voodoo traditions into their new Catholic beliefs. Longfield could see the local people looked and even dressed differently than most Afghans. Some of them had blondish and reddish hair and seemed almost Caucasian. They appeared even more rustic in appearance than the other Afghans he had seen, and Longfield hadn't thought that possible.

When he first arrived in Afghanistan over two years before in June of 2003, he felt like he'd stepped back over 2,000 years into the Old Testament. He still felt that way. Longfield assumed the women here would be even more covered up, if and when he saw any. It was extremely rare to ever see an Afghan female outside a large city because Afghans were extremely protective of their women. The sergeant was aware of how the houses here even looked different in structure. Longfield listened as his interpreter finished and drew his own conclusions.

"Nuristan is the West Virginia of Afghanistan," he said to himself. "These are Muslim hillbillies." The movie *Deliverance* kept flashing across his mind every time he thought of the toothless, grinning Afghan police officer. Longfield had been told to check out the possibility of getting a provincial reconstruction team (PRT) up here, but he didn't think there was anything to gain by having any Americans in Nuristan.

Oles discussed the cost of their bivouac with one of the local chieftains. Oles noticed his Terp was extremely nervous; that alone made Oles a little uneasy. The Terp wanted to pay the local officials the price they asked for without haggling or negotiating for a better one. Oles came to terms on a price for a little walled compound with two small buildings and two tiny outhouses that sat alongside the river. The elders said they would have it vacated immediately. Oles decided he'd make the bigger of the two buildings their Ops Center. It wasn't a very large compound but it was defensible, and it was surrounded by a six-foot rock wall (like almost every structure in Afghanistan). The wall provided some protection but, as the village was surrounded by mountains and ridges, it was not a safe place.

Rahim overheard they were paying for the compound and became visibly angry. He told Oles's Terp to tell the American captain they should just take the compound. Rahim said the money belonged to the ANA soldiers and the American had no right to spend it, especially on something they should take for free. Oles shook his head and asked his Terp to translate for him.

"We don't have too many friends right now," Oles said, looking at Rahim. "We don't need any more enemies. We need a place to set up our bivouac. We're going to pay for it and make at least one person happy with our being here." The ANA commander listened as the Terp spoke but he wasn't appeased. He moved off angrily and started speaking to some of his soldiers. They shot quick, angry looks at Oles.

Rahim was becoming increasingly antagonistic toward the ETTs. At first, he did not want to go to Nuristan. However, when the LTC showed up with the $1,000,000 Afghani for the mission, Rahim changed his tune quickly. He knew if the mission got scrubbed, the money would have to be returned. The ETTs felt Rahim hoped the mission would proceed, Dawson would spend very little of the money, and then when the mission was over, Dawson would hand all the remaining money over to him…to pay his soldiers. Dawson figured that meant Rahim would keep 95% of the money for himself, something Dawson would never let happen.

Dawson also discovered via radio back to BDE that the ANA LTC who had showed up with the money in Bari Kowt claimed to have handed $400,000 Afghani over to Rahim. When Dawson asked Rahim about it, he was evasive and refused to hand over the money.

The ANA began to set up their compound. Knowing the next day (the day before the election) would be a busy one coordinating with local chieftains, most of the soldiers worked quickly. Oles was told the village elders would be calling on them to offer support.

"Bullshit," he thought. Oles didn't believe that for a minute. He knew instantly they were coming to his compound to find out what their unit's troop strength and disposition was. However, it was their country, their village, and their army so, ultimately, Oles knew they were going to do what they wanted to do.

As everyone was tending to their duties, Oles noticed Midwest did not have his men setting up their machineguns and mortars yet. The American NCO was in charge of the ANA weapons platoon consisting of the Dshk (a 12.7 mm Russian machinegun similar to the American .50 caliber), mortar, and recoilless rifle.

"Hey," he said to Midwest. "Set up your weapons." Midwest started to slowly get his men moving. He looked as depressed and scared as anyone Oles had ever seen. Oles went into the adobe-style hut that would be their CP for the next five days and checked on his other American NCOs. They were all doing their jobs. They had their radios set up, supplies stacked in the small room, and an Ops center ready. Oles then went back to check on the weapons platoon again. He saw that Midwest had done a slack job of setting up his machineguns and mortars.

"What the hell," said Oles to him. "Readjust your weapons properly." Oles ordered the ANA troops to readjust every weapon. He noted Midwest didn't seem to care. The man was too scared. Oles was surprised that a US soldier could do such a poor job[11]. Especially in such a dangerous place.

The village elders arrived with the Afghan police and met with Oles and the two senior ANA officers. They spent the greater part of the night talking and discussing the situation. The village chieftain gave the normal assurances there wouldn't be trouble. He said his people would offer total cooperation.

It was then decided that the local police would be utilized to monitor the seven different polling sites spread out about 14 kilometers apart along the Nuristan Road surrounding Kamdesh. That would free up the ANA to be a QRF in case of any trouble and enable them to roll up in strength if they were needed. Otherwise, the ANA would be spread out, trying to protect all seven sites with a handful of soldiers at each site. It was insisted that the Americans keep a very low profile and stay in the compound while the ANA conducted their patrols and made the new government's presence known. Everyone was in agreement and the elders promised everything would go smoothly and peacefully.

They all shook hands and the police chief and village elders left. After their departure, one of the local policemen approached Oles's Terp and passed information he thought the Americans would want to know. The Terp casually strolled over to Oles and Longfield.

"The two men just leave your camp…one was Taliban and the other that leave before him was al-Qaeda."

"*What?*" gasped Oles in a mixture of disbelief and anger.

"*You're fuckin' kidding me?*" spat Longfield.

"You had Taliban and al-Qaeda here," repeated the Terp.

"Motherfucker!" said Oles aloud. Turning to the policeman, he said, "Why didn't you tell us? Why didn't you point them out so we could grab them?"

The Terp posed the question to the policeman. The Afghan answered in what sounded like jabber. Oles understood Dari but he couldn't discern this man's Nuristan dialect. The Terp turned back to Oles and said, "They did not want a fight. They did not want trouble."

"Great," said Oles. "So we can have trouble tomorrow."

Oles knew instantly that whoever those men were, they were reporting the news about the American/ANA weapons and troop strength to the local bad guys. But there was nothing they could do now. The two were long gone into the night. All they could do was wait and see what would happen. Oles ordered his ANA officers to put out additional security. Once everyone was settled in and the ANA were in their defensive positions with perimeter O-Ps, Oles made sure guards were set and everything was in order. Satisfied they were in as defensible a position as they could attain, he went to sleep himself.

Longfield took first watch with some of the ANA troops. It was unspoken, but the Americans never wanted to *all* be asleep at the same time. They never let the ANA know they felt that way, but they had decided that at least one American would stand watch at all times. Strate was still exhausted from the long sleepless week, and since Longfield was a night-owl who had difficulty sleeping anyway, he was the obvious choice.

Longfield made his rounds and thought of their situation. He didn't see it getting any better. Actually, with what he knew of the area and had been told by the SF, he was surprised they had not taken any casualties yet. Longfield waited out the long night checking the line and their O-Ps, returning to play Tetris on his Gameboy under a full moon. He could hear distant weapons fire, but it wasn't close and it was sporadic. He was relieved by Strate just before dawn.

The compound was awakened by gunfire. The incoming was ricocheting off the rocks maybe 100 meters from their buildings. The gunfire was from the distant cliffs down toward Mandagal, maybe 1,000 m away. It was AK fire and it was aimed at them, but it was inaccurate. The shooters were so far away Oles could barely see them. In answer, he told Midwest to register their recoilless rifle and mortars on the distant ridge from where the shots emanated. This was because the weapons needed to be registered, and he hoped they'd get lucky and get the shooters. It was also a good way to let any other would-be-snipers know if they got up on that mountain and fired on the compound, they would be hit with some 75mm or 82mm shells.

Oles ordered the mortar crews to drop two rounds up on the ridge and make some noise. He wanted to draw attention to the fact they had considerable firepower and would be eager to use it should they be messed with. Two loud "thunks" sent a pair of shells exploding atop the ridge. The incoming stopped immediately.

Satisfied with the mortars and not wanting to waste any more rounds, they registered the recoilless rifle. The crew fired two rounds and blew some rocks off the ridge where the gunfire had come from. It was a little like registering and a little like harassment fire. They hadn't done it the night before because they couldn't see the ridges. They didn't want to lob shells in the dark and perhaps blow up some farmer's house and infuriate the entire countryside. But now, with ACM, Taliban, or al-Qaeda obviously on the ridge, they let everyone know they meant business. Almost as an afterthought, Oles decided to send a presence patrol down the road to let whoever was shooting at them know a new force was in the area—and they were not to be taken lightly.

Two trucks with twenty ANA soldiers moved off and patrolled several kilometers down the road. The first patrol moved toward Mandagal and the Paki border. Then they returned and patrolled down to Kamdesh. While the patrol was gone, the bivouac was fired on several times from the surrounding cliffs. Once again, it was distant shooting from over 1,000 meters. It fell well short of their compound. Oles didn't waste any rounds in answer.

The ETTs and their ANA counterparts spent the long day watching and waiting for something to happen. The elections would start tomorrow and everyone was tense with expectations of trouble. However, the patrols returned and the day passed with nothing but intermittent AK fire from the cliffs, obviously aimed at their encampment. But the shooters were much too far away to fire with any degree of accuracy.

Late in the afternoon Oles was approached by one of the Terps. The ANA captain wanted to know what was to be done with their trash. Oles didn't know what to do with it and didn't really care.

"Bury it. Burn it. Who the hell cares?"

Dawson had been standing beside Oles, and he had a thought. By his own admission, Dawson would confess to having some odd thoughts from time to time. The NCO decided to make a raft. He would place the trash on the raft, set it on fire, and push it out into the river. Why? Even Dawson couldn't answer that unless it was because "surreal situations call for surreal responses." It just seemed like something interesting to do. With many quizzical looks from the ANA, Dawson began constructing a small raft with wood from the ration and supply crates. The Afghans were watching him, obviously wondering what he was up to. When the raft was finished, complete with a sail, Dawson placed it on the river's edge. He then set the trash on top and doused it with kerosene. One strike of a match set it afire. With the flames roaring, he pushed it into the river.

Dawson watched the current sweep the raft downriver and turned to see smiles on the faces of the ANA. Every one of them was watching, and most of them came down to the river's edge to observe the burning raft go further and further downstream. Some of them were laughing.

Oles watched the raft blazing as it sailed downstream and he cracked up, too. He noticed how the spirits of the ANA seemed to lift with Dawson's small act of arson. With dusk falling the flames disappeared from sight even as distant would-be snipers took pot-shots at them from the far cliffs. The bullets again landed well short of the compound. No one paid any attention to them except Midwest, who rarely came out of the building because of them.

Although the larger adobe hut was designated their "CP", more often than not, the American's CP was in the truck because that was where the radio was. Oles went to the Ford and called BDE HQ to report in.

"Saber 3, Saber 3. This is (Omega 6). Come in, Saber 3."

"This is Saber 3. We read you, (Omega 6), over."

Oles reported the day's events. He finished by asking HQ if they finally had written orders for them, or at least verbal instructions.

"*You guys are doing good,*" came the reply over the radio. It seemed to Oles they were ignoring the question. "*Keep it up. Hang tough. Over.*"

The first day ended without incident. The ANA guards were told to stay alert, and the compound settled into an uneasy night with sporadic AK fire and a few distant RPGs launched in their direction. None of the incoming landed close. It was obvious the shooters were more worried about return fire than they were about doing any real damage. But still, their harassing fire had made for a tense day for the Americans and their ANA comrades. The random incoming was a reminder they were in hostile terrain. The RPGs never even got within 400 hundred meters of them, but the explosions were evidence the enemy had very dangerous weapons and might work their way in closer to do some real damage. The AK fire ricocheted off rocks 100 m away or kicked up harmlessly in the river. However, everyone felt it was just a matter of time before the shooters got bolder.

With that in mind, the Americans got together for a meeting near Oles's Ford Ranger. Midwest was having a very difficult time keeping his composure. He wanted to leave Kamdesh and get out of there, orders be damned. All day he had stayed in their command building and only came out to use the outhouse. The others tried to calm him down but it wasn't working. Longfield tired of the sergeant's constant attitude of fear. It was time the man faced reality.

"This is a dangerous place to be a soldier," said Longfield, "We…"

"I'm not a soldier," interrupted Midwest, "I'm a mailman."

"Well then you need to give Uncle Sam all that money back they've been giving you for being a soldier." The others couldn't help but laugh. Longfield continued. He was talking to everyone but he was speaking to Midwest. "We are in a perfect place to die. We need to come to fuckin' grips with this because if we're going to die, we're going to die. If we're not, we're not. Just do your job as a soldier. If it's your time, it's your time, there's nothing you can do about it."

Midwest didn't like what Longfield had to say because he responded with, "But, what if it's not my time, but it's your time and I'm standing next to you?"

"Then it's your time, dumbshit."

Longfield might have felt sorry for Midwest if he wasn't so disgusted by his lack of composure. Longfield himself did not expect to return from this mission alive. He wasn't scared. He just felt that, as a soldier, the law of averages catches up to a man, and they were in the worst place Longfield had ever seen in his entire military service. This place had been bad from the first minute of the drive in. It was also the most primitive place Longfield had ever seen. For all he knew, it was the most primitive spot on the planet. Still, Longfield knew that, as a soldier, you had to expect situations like this and do the best you could, knowing tomorrow you might be dead. He flashed on the greeting they had gotten from the Afghan Policeman when they first arrived in Kamdesh—"Welcum-to-Nuristan. You Americans will die." Longfield knew that might well happen.

The only people he completely trusted were his fellow Americans and there were only four of them. But Longfield felt he couldn't count on Midwest. The man was too afraid. He wouldn't be good for anything. Midwest was making everyone else nervous because he was extremely irrational. Longfield's Terp had been the same way since their arrival. He always wanted to give everybody everything they asked for—be it money, food, or supplies. Like Midwest, the Afghan Terp wanted no conflict whatsoever.

Oles hadn't said much at the meeting. He mostly listened as his sergeants voiced their concerns. Dawson was angry at their higher. Longfield and Strate seemed resigned to their situation. Midwest was a wreck.

Oles was exhausted. It had been a long day. He imagined tomorrow would be even longer. The elections would begin so everyone was expecting trouble. Oles doubted they had the combat power to prevent the ACM from stopping the elections completely, but they would do what they could. He told everyone to get some sleep and took first guard. All five of them would rotate shifts so that one of them would be awake at all times. With that the Americans went to their billets and tried to sack out. Dawson scribbled the day's events in his journal. They had survived their first day in Kamdesh. Hopefully, tomorrow would be just as uneventful. If all went well, they could finish their mission and head back to Naray in five days.

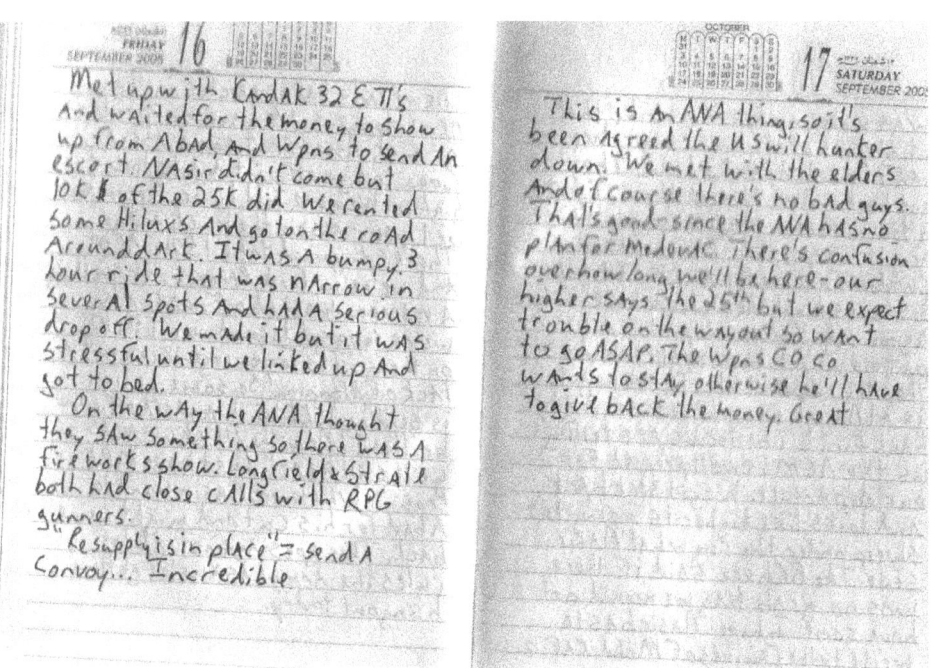

SSG Dawson's journal entries from September 16-17

"Everyone was covered in blood. One guys arm looked like a chicken bone when you're trying to get that last piece of meat," [12]

SFC Don Longfield

ELECTION DAY
September 18

Oles was up before dawn. He had managed to get about two hours of sleep. Election Day had begun, and an ANA patrol was preparing to go out. It was another presence patrol, and Oles was thinking about accompanying them. They were going to have a look around, but they were also going to let the locals in the area know the ANA was there in force. Oles had contemplated going with them because he needed to find a suitable landing site for a helicopter. He knew they would need a HLZ for re-supply and, at some point, they would probably have wounded. However, Oles decided to wait. The Americans were supposed to keep a low profile and stay in the compound. Oles decided to go out with a later patrol. He had his Terp call everyone together for the pre-patrol briefing. Even though he would not be accompanying them, he wanted to make it very clear as to what they needed to do. Oles's Terp was standing beside him, translating as he spoke. The ANA soldiers drank Chai tea as they listened.

"This is a presence patrol," said Oles, looking at the men as he spoke. "Have a look around, but let them know we are here. I want you to go a couple of kilometers down the road and come back." Oles listened as his Terp translated. He had worked with the ANA for over eight months and had begun to pick up the language. He could understand Dari enough that he didn't really need the interpreter to listen, only to speak. He could hear the ANA soldiers talking among themselves.

"These people aren't Muslim," said one, "We should kill them all."

"They aren't Muslim," agreed another.

Oles got the gist of what they were saying without the Terp telling him, but the interpreter didn't know that and told him anyway. "The men say we should wipe out the whole village," he explained. "These villagers aren't Muslim and they fear there will be trouble. We were lucky yesterday."

"You can't wipe out the whole village," said Oles in disgust. "We are here to protect the national elections, to ensure democracy. You can't just come in and kill people. Tell them that." The Terp echoed the captain in Dari, and Oles read by the looks on the faces that these ANA soldiers didn't care about democracy or equality.

The twenty-man patrol left the building and moved to the vehicles. They would take two pickup trucks. Oles went out with his Terp and the ANA lieutenant who would lead the patrol.

"Remind them to be vigilant," said Oles to the LT as the Terp translated beside him. "Talk to the local people and gain intelligence. Make your presence known. Patrol down to the polling sites."

It was dawn now, and Oles went back into the building to get the others up. The two pickup trucks rolled out and headed down the road. Inside, Dawson woke up feeling the need to urinate. He went outside but, instead of going to the outhouse, from habit he went over and relieved himself against the front tire of their Ford Ranger. It was something he did for good luck. Only, he was tired and wasn't paying attention. His stream hit the tire and bounced back on his boot and pant leg. He only knew it when he felt the wetness through his BDUs.

"Damn!" he muttered as he turned and went back inside. He was still tired and lay down to go back to sleep. Suddenly, everyone heard a tremendous explosion. It was different from the RPG blasts of the day before and louder, though farther away.

"GET UP!" bellowed Oles at everyone in the CP. "GET UP!" Then he took off running toward the sound of the explosion. His rifle in one hand, Oles ran down the road toward a cloud of black smoke rising from the direction where the patrol had driven. It had only been two minutes since they had left, and the smoke looked to be only some 800 m away. Oles's first thought was the patrol had detonated a land mine.

"IED!" he shouted back to the others as he ran.

In the makeshift Ops center, the others were scrambling up behind him. Longfield, Dawson, Strate, and Midwest were grabbing their weapons and combat lifesaver bags. They had their interpreter tell the ANA LTC to have his men prepare for an attack. The explosion might be the diversionary prelude to an assault from the opposite direction. The ANA were to keep a vigilant perimeter and expect an attack. With that the ETTs were out the door. They could see Oles running. He was several hundred yards down the road already. They made a quick plan. They would get the compound ready for an attack, then get in a vehicle and follow Oles.

Oles was breathing hard by the time he reached the ANA patrol and their two vehicles. He saw there was now only one vehicle and the smoking hulk of the other. The lead pickup had obviously hit an IED. The blast appeared to have been mid-chassis because the force had bent the truck-bed upward into an inverted V. The other vehicle appeared okay. The ANA who weren't wounded were standing around in shock. Several lay stretched out on the ground, unmoving. Half a dozen others were screaming and writhing in pain. All of the wounded were bleeding and burned.

Oles saw the LT in charge of the patrol and ran toward him. The Afghan was very excited and shouted over to him in a mixture of Pidgin English and Dari. The officer told him the first pickup had struck an IED buried in the road. They had one KIA (killed in action), seven WIA (wounded in action), and one MIA (missing in action).

Oles noticed the ANA from the undamaged vehicle were coming out of their shock. They were doing a good battle drill. They had spread out to in a defensible position, securing the area while the medics and a few others loaded the wounded onto the surviving truck. Oles figured the MIA must have been blown off the cliff into the river below because there was no sign of him anywhere. They quickly loaded up the injured, climbed aboard the remaining truck, and headed back toward their bivouac. The ANA soldiers who were not wounded followed behind on foot.

Oles was certain the patrol had hit an IED. There were no incoming rounds and he hadn't heard anything but the explosion. Checking the wounded packed in the small truck, he saw all of them had multiple lacerations and blast injuries. A few had traumatic injuries with hunks of flesh blown from their limbs. The pickup covered the distance quickly, arriving minutes later back at the buildings. The surviving ANA were jogging behind on foot.

Longfield, Strate, and Dawson had organized the ANA in the compound for a follow-up attack and were just climbing in a vehicle to drive to the IED site when the Hilux pickup approached, full of wounded. Dawson saw the bloody carnage in the truck and turned to Strate with his Skoal in one hand and rubber gloves in the other.

"Glove up!" he said as he stuck some chew in his mouth. The last time he had treated casualties, it had taken "too long" to get the bloodstains off his hands. Strate took a pinch of Skoal and quickly donned his own rubber gloves.

The truck came to a stop just outside the compound. Dawson, Strate, and Longfield ran over to help. The wounded were quickly unloaded and the ETTs worked on them right outside the gate. The first man Longfield reached had his bicep blown off. Dawson immediately applied a tourniquet while Longfield tried to figure out how to splint the arm to keep it stable and avoid as much pain for the man as possible.

The arm reminded Longfield of a half-eaten chicken drumstick. The man's hand and forearm were fine but his bicep and triceps were simply gone. All that was left was the bone of his upper arm with a few blue veins connecting the flesh of the shoulder to the forearm.

Strate was assessing casualties still in the bed of the truck. Oles was on the radio trying to arrange medevac. He looked down and saw Longfield and Dawson working on a man. To Oles, the soldier didn't look too bad. With so many other badly wounded men, Oles couldn't figure out why his sergeants were hovering over a slightly-wounded man. Then Longfield moved the tattered cloth of the ANA soldier's blown up sleeve, and Oles unconsciously gasped, "Holy shit!" The arm was gone where the bicep should have been. All that was left was a shiny white bone with a single strand of tendon and a few blue veins. Strate and Dawson were heatedly discussing what to do for the man. They decided their only option was the tourniquet and began securing it.

While they worked, Dawson felt a mixture of emotions. These were his men. Private Mohammad Hussein was lying beneath him with his arm rightfully blown off. Dawson felt sorrow for his soldier. At the same time he felt anger toward the coward who had done this and disgust toward his own higher HQ for putting them in this position. He was also experiencing doubt.

"Will this tourniquet work or not?" he asked Longfield. To him, Hussein's arm looked gone. He repeated the question to Strate.

"I don't know," replied Strate.

Oles listened to the sergeants and noticed there wasn't much arterial bleeding. He assumed the traumatic amputation had caused the veins to constrict temporarily.

"My two cents worth of input," thought Oles, "which isn't worth a fuckin' cent, is that the arm is gone." Oles thought they should put the tourniquet on what was left of the guy's arm near his shoulder and try to save his life. Longfield and Dawson had already done that. Oles knew the real challenge would be moving the man without yanking his arm off. The soldier was calm. Most of the other wounded were hopping around, shrieking in pain, but this man was quiet.

Oles noticed the guys with the least-severe injuries were screaming the loudest. All of them had lacerations from glass and shrapnel. Everyone had residual burn wounds. One of the worst of the wounded was a man with a leg wound. Everything from the man's knee down was minced meat. Longfield was certain they'd have to amputate. The wound was equally as bad as the arm wound.

Longfield became aware of his Terp, Mustafa, kneeling beside him. The Afghan was scared and consistently repeating, "We should just give up. Let us just give up." Longfield thought his Terp's comments were pretty bizarre and he had no confidence in the man. He tried to stay focused on the wounded but he also kept looking around. Longfield was even more concerned about a follow-up enemy attack. If the rest of the ANA were like his Terp, they could get wiped out if they were hit. Longfield noticed all the ANA were now gathered around the wounded. They were like people gathering around a car accident to see what had happened.

"Have the ANA set up a battle drill," ordered Longfield to Mustafa. "Tell them to set up three-hundred sixty degree perimeter security."

The Americans were working quickly, trying to get the wounded immediate treatment and save their lives, but at the same time they had the hardest time getting the ANA soldiers who were not hurt to keep perimeter defense and focus their attention on the surrounding heights. The Americans knew if the enemy were smart, they would strike during this confusion.

Longfield was checking the injured soldiers. He moved around continually to make sure the seven men who were wounded received medical attention. He worried an untreated man with a routine wound might slip into shock and die. He also checked for any additional, untreated injuries that might have been missed. It was very difficult to get the triage area organized. With the exception of the two future amputees (the horrific arm and leg wounds) the ANA wounded kept moving and rolling around in pain. Longfield couldn't keep track of them and would accidentally keep checking a man he'd already treated.

"Help me get them organized!" he said to the ANA medic. "We need to get the wounded organized!" Longfield knew they already had one dead man. He feared others might bleed out if they weren't treated in time. He came upon an unconscious soldier and began checking him for vital signs. The man had none. He was dead.

"Oh, no! We've got another KIA," thought Longfield. But then he realized it wasn't another KIA. It was the same dead soldier he'd already seen.

"Hey!" he called over to the medic. "Separate this dead soldier from the others or cover him up!" Longfield moved on to the next man. The soldier was howling in pain. He was cut and burned but his wounds were not life threatening. Longfield moved on to the next. Since he didn't speak Dari very well, he simply talked in a calm voice. He knew the men were panicked and needed to calm down.

Dawson glanced over at the dead man Longfield had told the ANA to separate from the others and recognized Mohumad Rafiq. The Afghan had been a good soldier. Now he was dead. Dawson again felt a smoldering anger. Not just at the enemy who had done this, but at his own chain of command for sending them out the way they had.

Oles felt he had a million things to do. First, he was worried because it was getting increasingly difficult to keep the ANA alert and on perimeter guard. They were watching the wounded, who were still screaming and writhing in pain. Oles kept shouting at the Terps to tell the ANA to pull security and watch their surroundings. The ETTs seemed to be the only ones concerned about security. They had to treat the wounded and at the same time be ready for an attack. It suddenly dawned on Oles that they had just lost 14% of their total combat power. They only had 67 men to begin with, and they'd just lost nine. If they got hit again, it could get ugly.

Oles knew they needed medevac right now, or two of the ANA would probably die. But they still didn't have a site adequate for a helicopter to land. Oles had meant to find a spot that day although he was glad he hadn't gone out with the patrol to look for it. However, they needed it now more than ever. He remembered the only helicopter landing site he had seen was in Kamdesh proper, about 10 km away. On the long, slow, dangerous Nuristan road, that meant an hour away—if they made it without coming under attack or detonating a second IED. They needed someplace immediately. Oles had noticed several spots on the way in where it might be possible to land a helicopter, but he hadn't checked them out yet. Without thinking, he broke into a run, moving down the road.

Longfield came upon another unconscious man who lay burned and covered in blood. The wounded man looked dead. "Did he bleed out?" thought Longfield. He was frustrated because he couldn't get the ANA wounded to stay still, and he had checked several men twice before others had been treated even once. Then he noticed the dead man was the same guy he had already checked, twice.

"WHAT THE FUCK?" he shouted to the ANA medics. "SEPARATE THIS DEAD SOLDIER FROM THE OTHERS OR COVER HIM UP!"

Longfield wanted to put all of his efforts into those he could help. The two amputee cases were lying quietly, but the other six wounded continued screaming and writhing around the lone dead soldier who lay among them. There was a lot of blood. It was a scene of chaos.

500 YARDS FROM THE COMPOUND

Every time Oles thought he found a site suitable for landing a helicopter, it turned out to be too small or too narrow. But each time he thought he saw another spot just a little bit further down the road. Then Oles saw a cornfield. It was very small but it looked large enough to land a Blackhawk on. Suddenly, Oles stopped. He looked back. He realized he was a good 500 meters from their compound. It dawned on him just as suddenly that it was not a good idea for him to be alone so far away from the others.

THE ANA COMPOUND

Longfield was wiping blood off a wounded ANA soldier's scalp. Both he and Dawson had ANA blood staining their uniforms. Longfield was trying to check the extent of the man's wounds when Mustafa approached him with an Afghan Police officer.

"He say they are picking up IEDs on the road," said Mustafa, gesturing to the Afghan policeman. "He say shit being blown off the road." Longfield looked for Oles to share this latest information with him, except he couldn't see him.

"Where the fuck is Captain Oles?" he said. He had just finished putting a dressing on the mangled arm. Strate was about to start on the same man's head wound.

Dawson looked around.

"I don't know."

A Terp who was standing nearby pointed down the road. He told them Oles had run off in that direction.

"What the fuck is Captain Oles doing?" said Longfield. He grabbed his rifle and moved to get a better look down the road. On one of the distant northern cliffs someone was cracking off potshots at them from 1,000 meters. Other than that it was eerily quiet. Longfield and Dawson realized Oles had gone down the road alone. They immediately ran to their Ford Ranger. They left Strate and the ANA medic to finish with the wounded. Dawson turned to Mir Zaman, the

Weapons Company 1st Sergeant, and shouted for him to send security down to assist them. Then he and Longfield drove off to find Oles. They weren't worried about IEDs because they wouldn't drive any further than the still smoking destroyed vehicle 800 meters down the road.

Oles didn't like being so far from the others but he had found a spot he felt was large enough for a Blackhawk. He started pacing off the perimeter. It was sufficient. He finished and turned back for the compound. He saw Longfield and Dawson driving toward him in the Ford Ranger. They linked and Oles told his sergeants about the landing site and his plan. Then they heard rifle fire from the southwest cliffs. Someone was cracking off rounds at them with an AK from over 900 meters away. Longfield told Oles they were taking fire from the north, too.

Oles used the truck radio to call Task Force Phoenix 1st BDE/201 Corps. He couldn't raise 1st BDE, so he called 2nd BDE. He gave Coen a SITREP (Situation Report) and "9 line" and requested immediate medevac. However, Coen said 2nd BDE didn't have any help to offer. He said he would try to get medevac from somewhere. Coen told Oles he'd get back to him as soon as he located something.

The SF then came on the radio. As usual, they had been monitoring the radio net. Oles told the SF OIC what had happened and overheard an SF soldier in the background say, "Oh, shit! Those guys are screwed!" Like Coen, the SF couldn't promise assistance either, but they told Oles they'd continue trying to get medevac from somewhere. Oles got off the radio.

In the meantime, the ETTs needed to secure the landing site. They drove back to the compound and met the squad Longfield had ordered to be ready. Oles called over to his Terp to have ten ANA soldiers accompany him back down the road. They were going to prepare the field for landing. Oles and the ANA ran back down the road to the field. It was a tiny plot of tall corn. Oles had his Terp instruct the ANA to start chopping down the crops.

"NAY! NAY!" shouted a livid old man. He seemed to appear out of nowhere.

"What the fuck is this?" said Oles to his Terp. "What does he want?"

The Terp went to the civilian and found out he was the owner of the field. He demanded they get out of his field or pay him for it. In the ensuing argument Oles deduced two things: one, the old man recognized opportunity when he saw it. He wanted money and lots of it. And two, he definitely did not want them to leave his field and go find another.

Oles felt the farmer didn't really care about his crops and "he certainly didn't give a shit about his wounded countrymen." Oles, his Terp, and the old Afghan farmer came to terms on a price for the field. By now Rahim had come down with several of his soldiers. He arrived in time to witness the transaction for the field and was seething. Rahim seemed to consider it ridiculous to pay for anything. Since the purchase of the compound the day before, any time there were bills to pay, he wanted to handle it. The Americans suspected he wanted to pocket the remaining money. But it had already been decided that Dawson would settle all accounts directly with the vendors or locals. The incensed Rahim watched everything with growing anger.

Longfield told several ANA soldiers to begin chopping down the field. They needed to make the landing site suitable and at the same time ensure there were no rocks or other debris that could be thrown up by the prop blast and damage the chopper.

Oles put security out for the HLZ and sent orders to have the wounded driven down. Then he got back on the radio to see if the helicopters were on the way. He called TFP 1st BDE/201 Corps because he was in 1st Brigade. But he was told that although he was in 1st BDE, his battlegroup was now attached to 2nd BDE/201 Corps, so he'd have to contact them. Oles radioed 2nd BDE and got someone other than Coen. The 2nd BDE staffer told him that although he was attached to them, he was intern Op CON-ed (Operations Control) to 3rd BDE attached to the 2nd Battalion of the 3rd Marines. This was because he was operating in Marine jurisdiction. If he wanted medevac, he'd have to get it from the Marines. Oles was frustrated, but he now felt action would finally be taken. Being a former Marine, he had a lot more faith in the Marines than in the Army.

However, when Oles contacted 2nd Battalion/3rd Marines, he was told he was in an area not controlled or operated by the Marines. The Marines suggested since it wasn't American troops who were wounded, they should call the ANA Air Force. It was their men and their country.

Oles radioed the ANA Air Force to get them to rescue their own wounded but was given a negative. The ANA Air Force flat-out refused. They would not fly into Nuristan.

With no medevac plan, it was a rigmarole of questions as to who would take the medevac request. Oles knew if the wounded had been American, there would have been a greater urgency from the other end. However, the wounded were ANA, and no one wanted to fly into Nuristan—especially the ANA. Oles again tried 1st BDE. The answer was no. Then he radioed 2nd BDE again. Nothing. He tried the 3rd Marines a second time. No. He tried the ANA Air Force again. No. Oles could get nothing but denials and excuses from his many radio pleas.

2ND BDE HQ's

Coen was monitoring the events in frustration. All their concerns were playing out. Coen was glad there was no American wounded. He was making calls to find any air support possible but was having no luck getting anything. Either there were no assets available, or they were too far away, or they were in another unit's AO, or they simply refused and said, "No!"

Kamdesh

Longfield looked around to see if the ANA were pulling security and saw there were now a lot of civilians gathering to watch what was happening. There were thirty or forty of them and they were maybe 50 meters away, absolutely fascinated by what was transpiring. Longfield had no idea where they came from. They seemed to appear out of the trees. He turned to Dawson and said, "I don't think anybody in this fuckin' town is voting. They're all here watching us."

Dawson chuckled and moved over to his ANA, issuing orders for them to close down the road at the southernmost point. He worried some ACM bad guy would sneak in to mingle with the crowd and then hit them with an RPG at point-blank range.

By now almost two hours had passed, and the casualties were getting worse. Two of the routine cases were now urgent because they were in shock and had been bleeding since they were hit. Oles feared they would bleed out before the chopper arrived. In addition, the unit had used all their combat lifesavers. There was still blood everywhere, and Longfield, Dawson, and Strate were stained with it. Without lifesavers Oles knew if they got hit, they had nothing left to treat the wounded, including themselves.

It startled to the Americans to realize they had used all their medical supplies treating the wounded from one blast. They had only been in Kamdesh a little more than twenty-four hours. And they were to remain there for four more days. On top of that, they were still taking AK fire from a mountain cliff 1,000 meters away. Dawson had been manning the radio since Oles's initial call, but Oles got back on to check for medevac. He was a calm guy and had been trying to remain calm on the radio, but he began to lose his temper.

"What the fuck!" he said into the radio. "These guys are going to bleed out. They are dying! We have no more IVs. No more quick clot. No bandages. We've got nothing fuckin' left! Get someone in here to get them out and bring us some more lifesavers!"

Longfield didn't blame anyone for not wanting to fly in and get them. At that very moment they were taking rifle and PKM machinegun fire from the cliffs to the northeast and southwest. Bullets were ricocheting off rocks sometimes only 100 meters away; some of them key-holed in their direction. Everyone knew the Taliban had surface to air missiles. The ANA were returning fire to try to keep the shooters on the distant cliffs suppressed, but Longfield noted they were just wasting ammunition. To add to the chaos, some of the ANA were firing RPGs. The distant explosions thundered down the valley and echoed off the cliffs. The civilians were watching everything in utter fascination. This was obviously more excitement than they were used to seeing.

Oles handed the radio back to Dawson and helped clear the landing site. He seethed at the stupidity of the mission. The SF had told everyone it was a bad idea. That alone said everything. And as usual, they were right. Oles feared the entire unit would meet the same fate as the SEAL team in Operation Redwing.

When the field was cleared, he went to check on the wounded. It took him a little while to reach them. While he jogged back up the road, he took in the situation. Bullets and small arms fire seemed to pop up from all directions. Explosions occasionally flared up, and Oles wondered if they were taking RPG fire. He could see the ANA firing their RPGs, but were the Taliban firing them, too? Oles wondered why the ANA would fire RPGs unless the enemy had worked in close. The situation was growing more chaotic by the moment. He asked the first ANA officer he came upon about the RPGs. It was the LT who had taken out the patrol that morning. He had no idea what was happening.

Oles reached the triage area and looked around at the wounded who were stretched out, covered in blood. He kept assuring them in his best Dari that help would come. Two of them were bleeding out in front of him, and there was nothing he could do. More than three hours had passed since the IED had decimated their patrol, and Oles still had been unable to procure medevac for the wounded soldiers. No one was willing to help them. But Oles kept trying. The only people who did not seem reluctant to talk to him on the radio were the SF.

Jalalabad

Combes was in the J-Bad TOC listening to the ETTs in Kamdesh over the SATCOM. It was the most frustrating two hours of his military experience. He was one hundred kilometers away, unable to physically do anything. He could hear his fellow Americans calling for help, but he couldn't get them any. He had been trying unsuccessfully for the last two hours. He wanted to saddle up and drive to Kamdesh himself but, of course, he couldn't.

"Hey," said the colonel, "You've got to just keep doing what you're doing so we can at least relay what's going on there. We've got to push what assets we have to these guys."

It was killing Combes! He had never been so frustrated and feared the ETTs were in for a bad fate. He kept getting on the radio, trying to locate medevac for them. From past experience, when he needed help, he called the Marines.

"Longfield was a guy they sent out cuz they said he was a trouble maker...but the colonel he told to 'fuck off', 99.99% chance that colonel had it coming. Longfield said it like it was...He was just brave as fuck, he had no fear."

LTC Patrick Coen

MEDEVAC ARRIVES

Three and a half hours after the IED explosion, Dawson got a call from Combes at 2nd BDE HQ. The Marines were sending a Chinook. Shaking his head because he knew the huge helicopter would never be able to land on their tiny HLZ, Dawson informed Oles of the news. Longfield was standing nearby and he was so frustrated he began laughing at the idea of a huge Chinook trying to land anywhere in Nuristan.

"A Chinook," said Oles incredulously as he took over the radio. "Negative! It's got to be a Blackhawk. A Chinook will never fit. It's going to be tight for the Blackhawk." As soon as he spoke the words, Oles knew he'd said the wrong thing. He feared they would now hesitate to send the Blackhawk if they thought it was dangerous. Combes signed off and said he'd get back to them.

Not five minutes later, true to his word, the radio squawked and Oles took an incoming call from Combes.

"Alright, package is on the way; two Blackhawk's, two gunships, and an A-10. Out."

Asadabad

Coen had been listening in the command center and heard Combes talking to the 2/3 Marines. The Marines were sending medevac to Kamdesh. Although Coen was in 2nd BDE, they were operating in Task Force Devil's battlespace. They were relegated to standing by. Coen called the 2/3 Marines and said, "We've got to push medical supplies to those guys!"

"We don't have any," came the reply.

"How do you not have any?"

"We don't!"

From Oles's repeated requests for more medical supplies, Coen knew the ETTs needed all the lifesaver bags they could get. But 2nd Brigade didn't have any, either. None. Coen grabbed his own CLS bag and hurried to the HLZ. His personal bag was loaded to the brim and equal to two combat lifesavers, enough to treat four severely-wounded men.

The Blackhawks were already warming up and preparing to move out when Coen ran up and handed over his CLS bag. He told the pilot to give the ETTs his bag and any extras they had.

"We don't have any!" the pilot said.

Kamdesh

It had been just over three and a half hours since the patrol had struck the IED. The ETTs began loading the wounded onto the undamaged truck for the five hundred yard drive to the HLZ. Oles was amazed at how quickly help arrived once they got the call from Combes. It wasn't fifteen minutes later when they received a call from the Marines saying medevac and CAS were two minutes out.

"Is the area secure and are you taking any enemy fire?" asked the Task Force Devil radio operator. Oles paused. They had been taking fire all morning from the ridges to the northwest and sporadic fire from southeast, but it had been ineffective. Oles's ANA security squad had been engaging the shooters to the north all morning, keeping them busy. Oles had the feeling that if he mentioned the small arms fire, the helicopters wouldn't land.

"There is enemy in the vicinity," said Oles. "But they are suppressed."

"Roger that."

Oles wondered if he'd just ruined his career. What he said was debatable. However, he justified his statement with the knowledge that the enemy gunners firing on them were too far away to be much of a threat with their AKs. None of their rounds had landed within 100 meters of the HLZ. Oles figured the danger to the Blackhawks was minimal, and the lives of the ANA outweighed the risk. Yet, it made him make another decision. Knowing he had to keep at least one squad back defending their base with all their supplies, Oles called to their bivouac and ordered another squad to come down and help pull security at the HLZ.

The A-10 came in first. It roared overhead and thundered by to check out the area. Oles listened to the radio and heard the A-10 pilot tell the helicopters it was okay to go in. Then the gunships came in. Like the A-10, they came in to check out the area. When they determined it was safe, they radioed the Blackhawks and gave them the okay.

"The helicopters are coming in," said the voice on the radio. *"You need to switch to FM to talk to them."*

Up to now all communication had been with BDE. However, with medevac and CAS on station, the ETTs needed to switch to direct commo with them. Longfield went to change his radio to the suggested FM mode. The original radio he had was the TACSAT, but after almost four hours its batteries were dead. He was now using Midwest's secure Army-issue radio The birds were on the same secure radio net but they were on FM. Longfield couldn't figure out how to change the radio to FM, so he called Midwest to ask him. Longfield hadn't seen him since they first scrambled out of their CP four hours ago. He called Midwest on the store-bought hand-held radio they all carried.

"(Midwest), pick up."

"Yeah?"

"Look, we need you to come down and get this radio up so we can talk to the birds."

"Where's Captain Oles?"

"He's trying to land the damn birds but we don't have coms with them."

"I can talk you through this."

"No, you need to get down here."

"Ah ... loo...ou're...brea...up. I'm...osing you..."

"Is he keying the radio on purpose to sound like the radio's going out?" thought Longfield. Then he repeated, "You need to get down here!"

Nothing. There was no answer. He tried again but Midwest did not answer anymore.

"SERGEANT LONGFIELD!" shouted Oles. "POP RED SMOKE!"

Oles assumed guidance on the Blackhawk and signaled the pilot in. Using his arms and hand signals, he attempted to give the pilot an idea of how close he was to the cliff. The pilot had a very small spot to land on and knew it. Oles could see the worry on the man's face. Too far one way, and his rotor would hit the cliff. Too far the other way, and he'd land on the cliff ledge and topple into the river fifty feet below. Oles had to stop him in mid-landing because his rotor was about to strike a brick wall on his right. He gestured for the pilot to pinwheel to get the chopper to fit. He couldn't hear him but he was watching the pilot and read the man's lips as he mouthed, "You gotta be fuckin' kidding me."

Oles mouthed back, "This is all we fuckin' got."

The pilot landed and the ETTs turned to get the wounded aboard the chopper. Strate and the ANA medic had IVs on everyone and were ready to evacuate them. However, before they could get the wounded off the truck, over two dozen ANA soldiers rushed the helicopter.

"WHAT THE FUCK ARE YOU DOING?" roared Oles at the surging group. "GET THE FUCK OUT OF THERE!" Oles turned to his Terp, "What the fuck is going on?" The Terp moved over to one of the ANA soldiers trying to board the helicopter and shouted over the noise of the roaring rotor. The man he spoke to wore a pained look on his face. He shook his head and shouted something back. The Terp turned back to Oles and said the man claimed to be sick. He said he had a splitting headache, needed medical attention and immediate evacuation.

"GET THE FUCK OFF!" bellowed Oles at the man. All the ANA who had rushed to board the helicopter were claiming to be sick. Now there were almost thirty of them.

"GET THE FUCK OFF!" roared Longfield again, thoroughly enraged. "WE'VE GOT WOUNDED THAT WILL BLEED OUT! GET THE FUCK OFF!"

All the ETTs were screaming at the ANA to get off the helicopter. Oles was worried the chopper pilot would get scared and take off before any of the wounded were loaded.

Longfield was in charge of loading the helicopter. He had a difficult time getting the wounded from the truck to the bird. The road ran through part of the field, and the helicopter took up both the field and the road. The long aft end of the chopper faced the truck. Worse, the ANA claiming to be sick with headaches and stomach pains were crowded between the truck and the chopper, blocking the way. It was narrow to begin with, one side being sheer upward cliff and the other a ledge with a sheer drop. The wounded had to be carried from the trucks to the Blackhawk through the chaotic group of ANA.

Longfield kept trying to keep security turned outward. From the moment the helicopters first appeared, the soldiers started watching them.

"PULL SECURITY!" he shouted. "PULL PERIMETER SECURITY!"

Longfield started grabbing soldiers and moving them in the direction he wanted them to face, pointing at his eyes and then motioning for them to watch the nearby cliffs. He ordered others to pick up wounded and carry them to the chopper. The ANA were so fascinated with what was going on that Longfield had to scream over and over to get them to do anything.

They loaded the wounded aboard the first chopper, fighting to keep the soldiers claiming to have sudden ailments at bay. Longfield was standing near the ANA medic when the Afghan asked the helicopter pilot for their medical re-supply. The pilot indicated it was on the other helicopter. The Blackhawk never cut its engines, and once the wounded were aboard, it lifted up and took off.

Since the first helicopter had made it, the second Blackhawk pilot wasn't as worried. The chopper came in and landed with more alacrity. Oles saw that his sergeants, Longfield, Dawson, and Strate, had done a good job prioritizing their wounded. Then it dawned on Oles—they were missing one American. Where was Midwest?

"Why isn't he down here?" said Oles to himself angrily.

The more severely wounded were on the first chopper heading for an Army hospital. The others were now being loaded into the second Blackhawk. Suddenly, the headache cases from the first bird started running for the second. Oles yelled for his Terp to order them off. They began arguing with the Terp. Using his poor Dari, Oles deciphered that the ANA were still claiming to be sick. The same man vehemently insisted he had a terrible headache and needed to be evacuated. Oles had his Terp order them all off. It took longer than he anticipated, but they finally got the ANA off and the remaining wounded on. Oles waved to let the pilot know he was good to go. The pilot opened his window and threw out a single combat lifesaver.

"YOU GOTTA BE FUCKIN' KIDDING ME?" Oles shouted back. The pilot just shrugged. He didn't have anything else to give. Then he shouted, "IF WE HAVE TO COME BACK, IT CAN'T BE HERE! YOU NEED TO FIND A BETTER LANDING SITE! WE'RE NOT GOING TO LAND ON THIS FIELD AGAIN! Then he lifted his bird and took off.

The helicopters disappeared over the mountains, and it became very quiet except for the distant AK fire. Dawson checked his watch. It had been three hours and fifty minutes since the IED blast, a long time to receive help. Oles looked to the ridges to the north and a smoldering anger began to burn in him. Throughout the entire time, from the moment the IED blew up to the present, Oles and his men were taking sporadic gunfire from the ridges to the northwest. It was ineffective fire, a few guys with AKs taking potshots from a great distance, but it was enough to infuriate Oles. He wanted to go up to Mandagal and retaliate. Oles had no doubt the shooters were from Mandagal and were responsible for the IED.

"Let's go get the fuckers," Oles said to his ETTs.

"Sir," said Longfield. "I'd like to get them as much as you, but we only have one lifesaver. We just lost ten guys to an IED. If we get engaged, we're dead."

Oles knew Longfield was right, but he was still angry. He was convinced it was men from Mandagal who had hit them. But he had already lost a squad, and he had to leave at least two squads at their base. That meant he had, maximum, three squads of infantry to hit back with. Not much combat power. He decided against retaliation. At least for now.

Oles was pleased with three of his NCOs. Longfield, Dawson, and Strate were good soldiers and they had worked hard. But Oles remembered the other NCO and thought, "Where the fuck is he?"

He recognized some of the men in Midwest's weapons platoon. He had his Terp ask one of them where the American sergeant was. One of the ANA soldiers tucked his hands under his shoulders and flapped his arms like wings. Simultaneously he clucked like a chicken. Another ANA soldier in the same weapons platoon said in surprisingly good English, "He up-a-da compound, scare-shitless!"

Oles was aware they had drawn spectators from the surrounding area. A few of the ANP arrived and spoke to Oles's Terp. The police said some locals had informed them the Taliban knew Americans were in Kamdesh, and the Taliban knew they lacked strength and numbers. The Afghan Police told the Terp that three hundred armed Taliban were coming to kill the Americans and their soldiers. Dawson asked Oles what the Terp had said.

"He said we're hosed and they're coming for us."

Then Oles noticed four unarmed and debloused ANA soldiers walking down the road. They were heading in the direction of Kamdesh.

"What are they doing?" he asked his Terp, knowing the answer. They were quitting. In the Afghan National Army, if a soldier wanted out, all he had to do was take off his uniform and lay down his weapon. He could quit the Army at any time. These four had simply taken their tunics off and laid their AK-47s down on the road. They were walking out, and there was nothing the Americans could do about it. Oles was glad there were only four leaving.

They had started this mission with sixty-seven soldiers. They had suffered nine casualties from the blast and just lost four more. They were now down to fifty-four men. And the remaining ANA wanted out as well. Even though only four men had quit, the rest of the ANA wanted no part of Nuristan and kept lobbying to their officers for an immediate departure. The civilian drivers were absolutely terrified.

Morale was extremely low. Obviously, from a combat standpoint, Oles's force was severely weakened.

At that point, with their small force Oles decided against sending out any more patrols. With only fifty-four men left, if they got in a fight or hit another IED and took more casualties, they would be in an even worse position.

The farmer who owned the field came up almost immediately after the helicopters had left. Dawson was in charge of the money so Oles had him pay the farmer. The man was ranting about something. Longfield asked his Terp to translate.

"He says you ruined his crop for the year. He won't be able to make it through the winter now. He is demanding money, compensation. He is demanding 30,000 Afghani ($800 US)."

Rahim turned to Longfield's Terp and spat something Longfield didn't understand. His Terp then turned and said, "He doesn't think we should give him anything."

It seemed a moot point to Longfield. Oles had already agreed to pay the man before the choppers even landed. Longfield figured the farmer thought they would renege on their payment.

"Well," said Dawson to Longfield, not realizing Oles had already made the agreement, "should I pay him that much?"

"Come here," said Longfield, taking Dawson aside. "Let's talk." When they got far enough away that no one could hear them, Longfield said, "This is what we'll do. Let's give him the $800 bucks because we are in the middle of fuckin' nowhere and we don't know nothing about these people. We've already been blown up once and we've only been here two days. We need to make some friends and try not to be pricks to anybody. But here's what we do. When we give him the $800 bucks, we tell him, 'This isn't for that one landing. If we need this son-of-a-bitch, we say two months, we are renting this frickin' field for two months.' That way, if we need medevac, or if someone comes in behind us, or we stay longer than we think, then we can land a bird if we need to. Okay?"

"Okay," agreed Dawson, but then he had a thought. "Since we're paying for the damaged crops, we should get a healthy dose of freshly ruined Afghan corn!"

They agreed and Dawson turned the money over to the owner of the field. The farmer now looked exceedingly happy to have had his field ruined. He said he would have his grandsons bring some corn up for them.

Rahim was furious. He had been watching and stormed over to Dawson and Longfield.

"Why are you paying for that field?" The Terp translated. "That money belongs to the soldiers. You should give it all to the soldiers."

"We can't just give it all to the soldiers," replied Longfield incredulously. "We've got to operate. This money doesn't grow on trees. This is all we've got. We've got to make it last."

Rahim was fuming and skulked off toward his troops. By now, the ANA were visibly terrified and did not want to stay in Nuristan a minute longer. But they were also killing mad. "Let us kill dem all," shouted one frustrated ANA soldier to Longfield in English. "Let us kill dem all and gedoud of here. Dey aren't Muslim."

Before they moved back up to the compound, Longfield pulled out a camera and snapped a photo of Dawson in front of the blown-up pickup truck. Dawson, ever the cynic, with a mouth full of Skoal, smiled and waved. They snapped a few more photos of the ANA in front of the truck. The Afghans looked extremely dejected. Everyone then turned and moved back toward the compound to get the ANA in security positions.

However, Rahim was so livid about the money issues, he told his ANA soldiers the Americans were squandering their funds and wouldn't let them have their money. The ANA, in turn, became furious and appeared to be starting their own revolution. Longfield was confronted before he even entered the compound.

"Why you pay so much for field?" demanded one ANA soldier. "Why you pay so much rent buildings?" demanded another. Everyone was talking and shouting angrily in broken English, Dari, or Posto.

"Oh my God," thought Longfield. "They are going to mutiny."

The ANA were enraged and didn't let up. "THESE PEOPLE ARE NOT EVEN MUSLIM," shouted another. "WE SHOULD KILL EVERYONE AND BURN THE VILLAGE!" All the ANA soldiers began angrily echoing that sentiment. "THEY ARE NOT MUSLIM!

WE SHOULD KILL THEM ALL!" Longfield and the other Americans tried to calm the ANA down, but they were so enraged at what their commander had told them, they were beyond reason.

From the moment they rolled into Nuristan, Longfield had felt he and the other ETTs were going to be killed by Taliban or al-Qaeda. But now he feared they might die at the hands of the ANA. The way the ANA were talking, since he and the other Americans weren't Muslim either, what was stopping the Afghans from killing them? The rage of the ANA was so great, Longfield was convinced he and the other four Americans were going to be shot and robbed of the remaining cash.

"You'll get your pay!" he told his Terp to promise them. "You'll get your pay!"

Only by being very careful and reassuring the ANA soldiers that they were going to receive their money were the Americans able to calm them down enough to go back into the compound and set up security. Using the Terps the Americans tried to explain to the ANA that for their own safety and well being, they'd better not make any more enemies while in Kamdesh. Especially not with the villagers. It was the ANA LTC, the one at variance with Rahim, who managed to calm his own men down. The ANA soldiers from his Kandak cooled off.

The men in Rahim's Kandak seethed but stalked off to glare angrily and talk among themselves. Longfield couldn't say what he wanted to say, which was, "Your commander's a dick-head," because the ANA soldiers' loyalty was to their officers and they weren't allowed to think otherwise. The ANA CPT was the real problem. Longfield thought it sickening that these men and their commander were more worried about their own month's pay than their dead and wounded comrades, two of whom would obviously lose their limbs.

The situation stabilized, but the relations between the ANA and the ETTs continued to be extremely strained. Longfield suggested to Oles in a low whisper, "Sir, we Americans better guard each other." Oles agreed and passed the word softly to Dawson and Strate. The additional bad news came as a death knell to Midwest, who was already having trouble coping with the situation.

Dawson was concerned about their money supply. As the pay agent he was doling out bills. Strate was, too, but Strate had twice as much money, and his Kandak CO wasn't giving him the headaches that Dawson's Kandak CO was.

Dawson had started the mission with only half the allotted amount. He had been paying for rented Toyotas, food for the ANA, rented buildings, fields, and they still had almost six days left in Kamdesh. He had recovered some of the money from Rahim but was still missing a very large amount. Dawson approached the LTC, hoping the Afghan officer could help him make sense of what was going on and to also get Rahim to be more cooperative. The LTC said if there had been no opportunity to make money, they wouldn't have been sent into Kamdesh.

Oles called a briefing with his ETTs and the ANA officers, including the LTC, Rahim, their XOs (both LTs). Because they were so weak in numbers, Oles had made a decision. They couldn't risk another IED strike, and with news of the Taliban coming to get them, they were now in a purely defensive mode and needed to stay together.

"We are not going to send out any more patrols," said Oles. "We're just going to set up O-Ps."

Even now the enemy appeared to be closing in on them. Aside from the potshots, they could hear voices being shouted down at them from the cliffs. Oles could hear his Terps and the ANA soldiers in their compound bellowing back up at the cliffs. The voices would echo off the ridges as they talked smack back and forth. The men on the cliffs announced themselves as ACM. They said they were going to kill everyone.

Oles had no idea how many of them were up there, but the rumors of three hundred enemy troops and the sporadic rifle fire they received from the ridges didn't give him any confidence that their situation was going to get any better. Oles was trying to stay positive and take the ACM presence in the hills around them with a grain of salt, but when the radio squawked with information from the SF, it became increasingly more difficult to keep morale up.

"*We've been monitoring radio traffic,*" said the SF OIC. "*Some asshole named Abulla just across the border from Pakistan has declared a jihad on the infidels in Nuristan.*" Oles knew he, Longfield, Dawson, Strate, and Midwest were the only infidels in Nuristan. The SF also said, "*There are three hundred volunteers coming across the border to hit you. You guys better stay alert.*" That was it. The evidence was corroborated. What had filtered in from the locals matched what the SF was telling them.

"It's going to be a hell of a fight," thought Oles. He felt they could hold their own right up until they ran out of ammunition. Even though they had loaded their vehicles with extra ammo, the ANA had already fired half of it. However, they had a lot of mortar and spigot rounds.

The day began to fade into the western skies and Oles and his men waited it out nervously, expecting to be hit. All afternoon the echoing taunts, slurs, and curses reached their ears as the ACM shouted obscenities at them from a distance. Gunfire would then follow as AK rounds were lobbed in, but it looked as though the shooters were content with harassing fire and the damage their IED had inflicted.

Oles could hear the distant chanting of the Muslims as they began their evening prayers. The chanting and praying was occasionally interrupted by gunfire from the cliffs. By now the gunfire was so common, the Americans (excluding Midwest) and their ANA companions weren't bothered by it unless the incoming rounds landed close by. More often than not, the harassing fire landed 100-150 meters off.

It had been a bad day. Morale was extremely low. Dawson looked down at his blood-stained uniform and remembered urinating on himself when his stream bounced off the tire earlier that morning. He turned to Longfield and muttered, "What a day! I pissed on myself and I'm covered in someone else's blood!"

"Be thankful it's not someone else's piss and your own blood."

Dawson thought for a moment about what Longfield said and realized it was true.

Oles noticed the large pile of trash from their blood-stained bandages, rations, and used supplies and remembered the raft Dawson had made the day before. For lack of something to do, he constructed another raft using more of the wooden ration crates. With the curious eyes of the ANA watching, he completed the raft, erected a sail, and took it down to the river's edge. Piling all the trash atop it in a large heap, he doused it with kerosene and set it aflame. In the last light of day he pushed the flaming barge out into the river and watched it float downstream. To the delight of the laughing ANA, who came down to the river's edge to watch it, the flaming raft again disappeared downstream. To Oles the ANA seemed like children with their volatile mood-swings. One minute they were furious, the next delighted.

Like someone pulled down a lampshade, dusk fell and the guardsmen settled in for their third night in Kamdesh. Dawson jotted down the days events in his journal as Oles went to his Ford Ranger to call headquarters.

"Saber 3. This is (Omega 6). Come in, over."

"*We read you, (Omega 6). This is Saber 3. How you guys doing?*"

Oles told BDE what they already knew—he had lost nine men to an IED and four more had simply taken off their uniforms, dropped their weapons, and walked out. Oles asked if they had anything new for him. When they said no, the captain asked when he could expect official orders for the mission and their extraction.

"*Be advised, we are formulating a comprehensive plan for your extraction. Hang tough, (Omega 6). Out.*"

Oles signed off and thought, "Good! Finally!"

Up to now BDE hadn't said anything about definite plans for the unit. "A comprehensive plan for extraction" sounded like they were finally going to give him something. Oles figured one of two things would now happen. They would either send an element up to Gowardesh to link with them and move back together, or they would send an element all the way in and link at Kamdesh. Then they would fight their way out. Oles knew their leaving route would be bad. The enemy knew there was only one way out, and they would be waiting for them.

Sergeant First Class Don Longfield

Photo taken near Kamdesh

A view of the river, the surrounding terrain, and a typical Afghan bridge

View from the ANA bivouac. Snipers on the distant cliffs kept up daily harassing fire.

One of the outhouses at the ANA compound

CPT Oles atop HMMWV; before entering Nuristan

The ANA compound and CP building (Cover picture)

Dawson beside IED-destroyed Ford Ranger. Also, ANA LT Ajmal, 1st Platoon leader.

Understandably dejected ANA troops

The narrow Kamdesh/Nuristan Road near the ANA bivouac.

Another view of the IED-blasted truck with the cliffs the ACM shooters fired from.

One of the ANA trucks with machinegun mounted on top.

View of the river from the compound near where Oles launched their flaming rafts.

"We knew there were bounties on us. There were always bounties on Americans. There were bounties on ANA officers and Terps as well but they weren't as much. And we were easy targets because there were only five of us."

SFC Don Longfield

THE ELECTIONS CONTINUE
September 19

Oles was up just before dawn. He'd gotten very little sleep. All through the night he had made round after round to the O-Ps, expecting an attack. Longfield and Strate had been up most of the night, too. There was no thought of sending out another patrol. The area was undoubtedly sown with IEDs, and the ANA couldn't afford any more casualties. As soon as the sun rose, the AK fire from the distant cliffs began anew. It continued to be ineffective, ricocheting off the rocks. It was harassing fire designed to keep them nervous and to prevent them from getting rest. It was working. At this point Oles felt they were just keeping their heads above water. He reiterated to his Terp to remind the men on security to stay alert.

The day began and the elections proceeded, but the ETTs and their ANA comrades didn't observe it. They were holed up in their compound, trying to stay alive. Except for a few vehicles and random pedestrians walking by their bivouac, they were alone in the world. There was very little traffic along the Nuristan Road, but every three hours or so a car would approach their check-point. It was usually a farmer in an old dilapidated 1980s vehicle that obviously had several hundred thousand kilometers on it, but there was nothing overtly suspicious, and the ANA always let them through. The Americans wondered where these drivers got their gas. There were no gas stations for hundreds of kilometers. The Americans and ANA had brought their own extra gas in big jerry cans in the beds of their trucks.

Around noon, Oles decided they couldn't just stay holed up for the rest of their time in the Kamdesh area. If the ACM knew how bad off they were, they definitely would attack. Oles decided to send out another presence patrol. This time they wouldn't go far and they would go very slowly, checking the road in front of their vehicles with metal detectors. Oles told his Terp to have the patrol drive only 1,000 meters down the road in either direction and then head back. They were to stay within range of the mortar and the recoilless rifle.

The patrol moved out and headed slowly down the road toward Kamdesh. It was a twenty-man patrol with two vehicles (two fifths of their total manpower). Several ANA Soldiers were moving carefully in front of the lead vehicle using two Sears & Roebuck beachcomber metal detectors to search for IEDs. The detectors were the kind that civilians used to find quarters on the beach. Oles was glad he had had the presence of mind to throw a few of them in the truck before they left Naray. They were extremely primitive, but he hoped they'd work.

They did. The patrol hadn't traveled 500 meters before they discovered another IED. It was even closer to their camp than the one from the day prior and had obviously been sown in the night. This time, however, they located it without detonating it. The explosive devise was an anti-tank land mine with a very primitive trigger. It was like the ballast for fluorescent lighting where the current runs through the bulb. Basically, it was a trigger wired into a blasting cap that sat on the pressure plate of the mine. It was extremely powerful. The enemy had buried the mine in the dirt road and had it hooked up to explode when someone nearby triggered it. The control for the trigger looked like a garage door opener. If someone pushed the button on the control, the battery was initiated, and the current ran through and detonated the blasting cap which then struck the striker plate on the mine.

Luckily for the ANA patrol, there was no one around to detonate it. Someone was probably supposed to be in a position of cover on a nearby ridge or somewhere else in visual contact, but he wasn't. Oles wondered if the delay on sending the patrol out saved lives. The two previous patrols had gone out in the morning. This patrol was in the afternoon. Oles wondered if the guy manning the control for the mine had given up and left or simply moved off for some reason, intending to come back. Regardless, it was very lucky for the ANA that it wasn't detonated while a mine-sweeper was standing on top of it.

Meanwhile, still wanting to recoup the money that was stolen, Dawson approached Rahim and requested the $200,000 Afghani that was still missing. Rahim said he didn't know anything about it and moved off. Tensions were very high. The ETTs held an intense dislike for Rahim, whom they considered a thief. The ANA LTC also held contempt for Rahim. The two were constantly fighting whenever they were around each other, and both men stayed on opposite sides of the camp within their own company areas.

All day Oles was aware the elections were supposed to be proceeding. The ANP came by twice to report the turnout was poor. Oles wasn't surprised because there were so few pedestrians moving along the road. He felt it didn't matter, either, and he believed the ANA and ANP knew it as well. To Oles, elections in this part of the country were as follows: the local villagers were told who to vote for by the tribal elders—and they did just that.

The patrol returned after picking up only the one IED. Then they headed the other direction toward Mandagal and the Pakistani boarder. What was so egregious was that several vehicles had already used the road that day. Did that mean everyone knew about the explosives except the ANA and the Americans? It seemed obvious. Certainly everyone in the area had heard about the IED from the day before and knew the Americans and ANA were targeted. They probably knew the ACM were letting everyone pass while they waited for another ANA patrol from the compound. But what Oles couldn't understand was why the man failed to detonate the IED. If he had done so when it was discovered by the patrol, he would have claimed at least one life with the blast and probably two. It didn't make sense.

The patrol then headed down the road in the opposite direction. They traveled 1,000 meters toward Mandagal but returned without picking up any IEDs. However, it did bring a reprieve in the harassing fire from the cliffs. Maybe the shooters thought the patrol would engage them or climb to look for them. Whatever the reason, they stopped firing. The soldiers turned around and headed back. Almost the minute they reached the compound, the shooters on the distant cliffs started up again. The ANA returned fire in the same sporadic manner.

An hour later, around 1500, the ANP showed up again to give the ANA the latest information filtering in from the locals. First, the road back to Gowardesh was now heavily mined. So there was no escape. Second, the rumor of the three hundred-man force coming to get them was incorrect. The actual size of the force numbered over four hundred, and the men coming to kill them were going to chop their heads off and place them on stakes lining the Nuristan Road.

This news understandably shook the ANA. They wanted out. Now! Oles felt the only reason the ANA force stayed together was because they were afraid if they put their weapons down and tried to walk out, they'd get taken prisoner and killed. The person who took the news the worst, not surprisingly, was Midwest. Oles felt kind of bad for him. A suicide mission in a remote corner of Afghanistan was probably not what the guy had signed up for when he first joined the National Guard. This certainly wasn't the monthly weekend excitement and extra money that Guard recruiters used to entice people to join. Oles had a difficult time getting Midwest to do anything that involved leaving the CP.

The Kamdesh elders showed up after the police left. They claimed the village of Mandagal was responsible for the IED blast and was heavy with ACM.

"Hell," thought Strate as he listened to the Terp translate for Oles, "when we got here, we asked you if there was any enemy activity in this area. You said, 'No.' Now, we have two dead soldiers and half a dozen wounded. Whose ass are you covering?"

The elders then pointed to a house right above the compound. It was across the river, very high on the mountain, maybe nine hundred yards away. They said that was where the Taliban was staying. The ETTs knew it would be very easy to blast the house off the side of the mountain with their recoilless rifle and mortars. Strate wanted to hit the house immediately. The others did, too, but they discussed destroying the house and came to the conclusion they weren't going to start trouble; they were only going to respond to it. They were already taking fire and verbal threats from the ACM but they hadn't heard from the

Taliban. And they didn't want to if they could help it. Maybe the two were infighting. The ETTs didn't want to force collaboration between the ACM and Taliban by blowing up the Taliban's lodging...at least not yet!

At about 1530, Oles was informed by his Terp that a police officer had just arrived at their compound with information about their missing ANA soldier. The explosion had killed one and wounded seven, but they still had one man unaccounted for. He was listed as MIA. The police chief told the Terp that a local villager had come in and informed him of the whereabouts of the missing soldier. According to the civilian, the wounded man was at a clinic down the river. Apparently, the blast had hurled him into the river and he'd been swept downstream. He was alive and in stable condition. All they needed to do was send someone for him.

"Okay," said Oles, turning to Longfield and Dawson. "Let's load up and go get him."

"Sir," said Longfield, "Let's utilize the assets we've got. Let's send the local police and some of the national police down to go get him."

Oles then thought, "This sounds fishy as shit." He turned back to the policeman and asked, "Where's the villager?" The Terp posed the question to the police chief. The man answered, "He left." Oles figured it was more like, "He disappeared."

"Is there a clinic down the road?" asked Oles. He didn't remember passing anything but a few huts and shacks. The Terp asked the police chief, who answered in a language Oles didn't understand.

"No. There's no clinic", translated the Terp. "There's just a few building that make up a little village."

"Can the police check it out for us?" asked Oles. "If he's there, we'll come get him."

The Terp posed the question to the Police chief and the man nodded yes. He turned and left. The day continued with the compound taking distant harassing fire but the rounds fell short.

Several hours later the policeman returned with a body in the back of his beat-up old truck. It was the missing ANA soldier. His name was Mohamud Amin. He was dead. Dawson looked down at the body of another one of his soldiers and felt rising anger. Amin had been one of his best squad leaders. It was because of Dawson the man had been an NCO. Dawson had seen Amin's potential and had sent him to the NCO camp at Kabul. Now he was dead.

Oles's Terp, Sayed Karam, went to talk to the police officer while Oles went over to check the body. Although the soldier had been dead for two days, there was very little decomposure. Oles assumed it was because the temperature of the river had kept the body almost frozen. Oles looked the corpse over and came to the conclusion that the blast had killed him. The man had died before he landed in the river.

They carried the body back into the compound and placed the corpse under a tarp in one of the truck beds. It was important for the Muslims to wash a dead man's body and bury it before sunset the next day. Oles was sending the truck back with a civilian driver, one of the few men Oles felt he could trust, and Mir Zaman, dressed as a civilian. Mir Zaman was the 1st Sergeant for the 31st Kandak, and he was picked to go because the ETTs trusted him.

Oles explained to Zaman that he had several tasks. He was to go back and obtain the other half of the money so they could continue their mission, and he was to try to acquire additional medical supplies and more food. It was hoped that one truck, driven by two men in civilian dress, at night, carrying a dead body, wouldn't draw too much attention and get attacked. What concerned Oles more was that they might run over an IED.

It was now toward the end of the third day. Oles was sitting on their O-P with one of Dawson's ANA soldiers. He was an older man, one of the few professional soldiers in the battalion. He had fought the Russians in the 1980s, the Pakistanis and the Taliban as a member of the Northern Alliance from the 1990-2001, and now he was in the Afghan National Army. He was a seasoned, grizzled veteran. Knowing he had been in some pretty tight spots before and thinking they were in a pretty tight one now, Oles asked the old soldier a question via his Terp.

"How do you feel about our situation?"

The man looked at Oles and shrugged. In broken English he said, "Ah…you know…we got guns…dey got guns…what happen

happen…it jus' wha' we do." The older soldier was very calm. Unfortunately, some of the younger ANA soldiers were not reacting as well to the stress and did not have the same philosophy as the old soldier.

"We need to kill all of them," said one of the younger soldiers to his comrades in Pashto. "They are not Muslim! They are not true Afghans."

The Americans had heard the same words so many times, they didn't need the Terps to translate. It was the most common expression spoken by the ANA soldiers since they'd arrived in Kamdesh. The Americans let the ANA vent. Confronting them about their remarks would only alienate them further, and they were already dangerously afraid. Also, most of them were still angry about the money situation.

All day long rifle fire could be heard. The shooters on the cliffs still seemed content to fire at the compound from unrealistic distances, and the ANA were content to return fire in the same manner. The report of weapons was so frequent the ETTs (barring Midwest) had begun to ignore it.

Just before dusk was sniper time. The ETTs and the ANA knew to stay low around dusk. The ubiquitous pot shots continued from the northern ridges, but that wasn't what the Americans were worried about. Their great concern was that the ACM would crawl closer and get into a position to do some real damage. One good sniper could do a world of hurt. Oles couldn't understand why the ACM didn't try to send someone in closer. He wondered if the mortar and recoilless rifle made them think about keeping their distance.

Just after dusk Oles's Terp came over and motioned to their large pile of trash. Knowing the smirks and laughter they got from burning the raft the previous days (and knowing it couldn't hurt morale), Oles decided to construct another raft and light it on fire. Dawson thought it was hilarious. He came out and stood among the ANA, laughing as they watched Oles construct a sail and attach it to the MRE crate which doubled as a boat. The Afghans watched with great interest as Oles placed all their trash on the raft. Oles noticed that even the old veteran got a kick out of it. Then Oles doused the raft with kerosene and lit it on fire. To the roaring delight of the ANA, he pushed the flaming barge into the river. Many of the Afghan soldiers again moved down to the water's edge to watch as the current swept the raft downstream and out of sight.

As if on cue, the sun disappeared behind the mountains. As he had the night before, after dusk Oles moved over to his truck to raise BDE on the radio.

"Come in, Saber 3."

Oles gave higher HQ a SITREP and then asked, "Saber 3, do you have a plan to extract us?"

There was a pause and then, *"Uhhhh, yes...will get back to you on that (Omega 6). Stand by."*

There was another extremely long pause. It was very frustrating for Oles. He was pretty sure it was equally frustrating for Saber 3.

After no less than a minute, Saber 3 came back on the radio. *"Be advised, captain, corps staff is drafting up a comprehensive plan to extract you and your soldiers. Be patient, we'll get you out. You guys are doing good (Omega 6),"* assured the voice over the radio. *"Hang tough."*

"Roger that, Saber 3. (Omega 6) out."

Oles got off the radio. The message was almost exactly what they had said the night before—they were "formulating a comprehensive plan for extraction." Oles wondered if they had done anything at all. He then called up the SF who was listening back at Naray.

"Did the package arrive?"

Oles was referring to the two men he had sent back in a truck dressed as civilians who were returning the body of the dead ANA soldier for burial.

"Yeah," came the reply. *"They put him in a casket and sent him on his way."*

Oles knew the SF had been monitoring their radio broadcasts since the day they arrived because they often spoke to him about them. Then the SF OIC gave Oles some intel that confirmed the latest news.

"You got four hundred enemy troops in the immediate area around Kamdesh. They know you're a bite-sized piece. They are sending guys from Mandagal to hit you."

It was very disconcerting to hear, but it was valuable intel. Oles knew not to send any patrols out beyond the range of their mortars and recoilless rifle. "Thank God for the SF," thought Oles when he got off the radio.

The captain knew they only needed to stay alive for two more days. They had orders to stay in Kamdesh for five days, and they'd already been there three. They would leave in the early morning hours of September 22. However, Oles was concerned with his supply situation. They were beginning to run out of food and water. They had long since run out of medical supplies, but they could keep going, barring another IED or firefight. However, without food and water they were going to find their difficult situation increasingly harder to bear. The ANA had begun to drink from the river, but doing so had already caused diarrhea with several men soiling themselves.

Oles was tired and after making rounds to the O-Ps he turned in for needed sleep. Longfield and Strate took the nightshift. Dawson wrote the days events in his journal and also tried to rack out.

SUNDAY SEPTEMBER 2005 — 18

Was woken up by a mine strike that hit AWPSS Co Patrol in a R Anger. We had 7 wounded, and 2 dead. They got here and we triaged them, I put a tourniquet on Mohd Husseinb but his arm is not operable. Then we had to cut down a fence for an LZ. It took 3.5 hours to get the medevac here - not a good sign for us. We pulled all patrols and told the police leaders they are responsible. The resupply is at Nariah so we have to send guys back for it. The locals are telling us the ACM is well prepped for our departure. We got 300k back and looks like higher is going to sweep under the rug what Nasir stole. The B Chere said if there was no grab bag we would not have come. I hope Nasir has to write to the families of Mohd Rafiq and Mohd Amin.

MONDAY SEPTEMBER 2005 — 19

Had a string of people coming in today to tell us how mined the return route is and how many bad guys are waiting. The soldiers are getting skittish, the 2 ANA officers are acting like children and they still have yet to give us the remaining 200k Afghani.

Corps is going to give us a "comprehensive exfil plan", even tho our tasking statement was all that got us here.

The ballots are collected, if we can get trucks + an answer of who will move them we might be out of here early the 21st.

SSG Dawson's journal entries for September 18-19

125

"Everything you are ever taught, or told, goes out the window because it's a political mission. We've got to have somebody up there to try to maintain the validity of the election or at least the appearance of the validity of the election. Think about it. Any Afghans in a leadership role [in Kamdesh] had to be Taliban or al-Quada or at the least they would have to conform, otherwise they would be killed."

LTC Patrick Coen

SURVIVING
September 20

The fourth day dawned and seemed even bleaker for Oles and his men. However, they hung on to the hope that if they could just survive another twenty-four hours, they could leave Kamdesh. Oles began the day by calling BDE. HQ had nothing except what Oles thought "was a bunch of bullshit" about all the good their presence was doing in Kamdesh.

Oles was pretty sure their presence hadn't done anything but stir up the bad guys. The ANA didn't do anything but keep security around their compound and send out a rare patrol. And the patrols never drove further than 1,000 meters in either direction because everyone stayed within mortar range. Since the voting sites were several kilometers away, Oles didn't see what good their presence could possibly be doing. In fact, they had drawn four hundred bad guys into an area they weren't in four days ago. Oles knew his force was entirely defensive. He supposed the enemy knew it, too, if they had any tactical sense. They had to know the few patrols the ANA sent out were just attempts at showing force.

Once again, a patrol moved out. It was another two-vehicle patrol made up of twenty ANA soldiers. They crept along, two men using metal detectors to comb the road for IEDs. The ANA followed with their eyes on the surrounding ridges. As on the previous day, they came upon another IED within 1,000 meters of their compound.

Having moved the intended 1,000 meters down the road, the patrol turned back toward the compound and repeated the recon in the opposite direction. When they had covered the same distance, they returned to their camp.

Inside the walled compound the remaining ANA and ETTs were bored like they had been since their arrival. Lacking something better to do, Oles, Longfield, Dawson, and Midwest decided to play cards. They paired off with Dawson and Oles on one team and Longfield and Midwest on the other. They usually played Hearts, but today they were playing Euchre. It didn't take more than a few games for Longfield to realize that his partner wasn't very good at cards. They were losing every hand even though Longfield was being dealt good cards.

Longfield tried to tell Midwest how to play more wisely, but the E-7 didn't seem to understand. Then the radio squawked with a message from BDE. Oles got up to answer it. Longfield and Dawson listened intently since any news concerned them. They wanted to know what BDE had to say.

"Hey," whispered Midwest to Longfield, "let me see your cards."

"What?" said Longfield. He had been listening to the radio.

"Let me see your cards," hissed Midwest under his breath, "quick." He gave a shifty glance toward Dawson to let Longfield know they needed to be covert.

"Dude, are you fuckin' cheating!"

"Shhhhhh," hissed Midwest, shooting a quick look at Dawson to see if he'd heard. Dawson was listening to Oles's conversation with BDE.

"Quick," continued Midwest, "before he (Oles) comes back."

"Dude, I'm not fuckin' cheating. You're an asshole. Fuck you."

Midwest was beginning to seriously grate on Longfield, who felt the guy had done nothing but complain and hide the entire time they'd been in Kamdesh. Now he was cheating. Being scared was one thing thought Longfield—a man didn't have much control over how he responded to combat—but cheating was a conscious effort. The man was chosing to be dishonest.

Longfield got up and went outside. He could tell brigade didn't have anything new. He pulled out his smokes. On cue, before he put the cigarette to his mouth, his Terp was beside him asking him for one. Longfield handed one over but feared the day he'd run out. That day was rapidly approaching, too, as he only had a few packs left. He'd started out with four cartons and he was down to two packs.

"Hey, Longfield," called Oles from the CP. "Let's finish the game."

"I ain't playin' no more."

"Why?"

"Cuz my teammate's a cheater."

"Well, come in anyway. We need to talk."

Oles called for Strate while Longfield finished his cigarette. As he did at least once a day, Oles gathered his American sergeants together for a briefing. After Strate entered the CP, Longfield followed them in. Oles explained their situation, telling everyone what they already knew. Things were looking increasingly bad. Oles felt it was only a matter of time before the four hundred bad guys who had crossed the border from Pakistan began to take a concerted interest in seeing them die. If that happened, Oles wanted to have a contingency plan. He gave instructions to the others if he should be killed and advised the survivors what they should do if the situation got desperate.

"I do not want my head chopped off my dead body on Al Jazeera TV for my wife and family to see," he told his men. When he said this, he noticed Midwest noticeably blanch and grow pale. The other sergeants nodded in agreement as Oles continued, "Burn any paperwork we don't want the bad guys to see and then take any of our dead bodies and burn us or throw us into the river." Oles looked at his NCOs as he spoke. Midwest looked like he was going to be sick.

"Fire or blow all the ammo. Don't let the Taliban get any of it. Throw it in the river if you have to, but destroy it. Lastly, get out. Any way you can. Follow the river if at all possible and make it down to Gowardesh." That was it. The briefing ended and everyone went back to doing nothing. Midwest went to his corner in what appeared to be demoralized shock.

Longfield went out to smoke another cigarette. The long day was wearing on him. Of course, his Terp was standing beside him bumming a smoke. It seemed to Longfield that whenever he pulled out his cigarettes, his Terp would suddenly appear next to him. While smoking, Longfield noticed a conversation between the ANA LT from Strate's Kandak and one of his sergeants. Longfield asked his Terp what the two were talking about. He could see the officer clearly because the man was facing him, but the other soldier was between them with his back to Longfield. The conversation was becoming heated. The Terp told him the soldier was complaining about not getting enough food. The debate continued until the LT accused the soldier of being fat and told him to stop whining. The soldier then made a disrespectful comment toward the officer. Outraged, the officer drew his pistol and aimed to fire.

"STAY IN THE BUILDING!" shouted Longfield to the others as he took cover. When the LT drew his pistol, Longfield was in the line of fire. Several other soldiers grabbed the officer and tried to calm him down. Others told the sergeant to leave the area. The man left, but he was still angry and shouted back over his shoulder as he stepped out of the compound. The situation was temporarily resolved, but Longfield wondered for how long. He knew this trivial disagreement had escalated into near murder because the ANA were so fearful about being attacked, be it IED or direct.

Longfield wasn't surprised when the truck driven by the ANA first sergeant returned. The man was a good soldier, which was why they had selected him. The ANA NCO and his civilian driver had returned the body and made the slow trip back carrying the needed food supplies. When the truck pulled up, Longfield and the other ETTS looked in the back and saw a large cardboard box two feet long ,one foot wide, and eighteen inches tall. It was filled to the brim with random boxes of medicine and loose pills. There were no combat lifesaver bags.

"What the fuck?" said Longfield, looking at the others. Everyone began laughing cynically. "What the fuck are we going to do with this?" posed Longfield, holding up a laxative. "What did they do, just throw anything they could find in a box?"

They brought the food supplies and medicine into the building. The food was Halal (Holy) meals—MREs for the ANA that did not contain pork or foods considered unclean by the Muslims.

The local elders showed up again. They promised continued support for the mission but asked for payment for the past days' support. Dawson reluctantly handed over 50,000 Afghani. The village elder said it was not enough. In an attempt to try to sweeten the deal and appease the man's obvious resentment, the ETTs threw in a box of medicine from the new cache the ANA 1st Sergeant had brought back. It didn't work. The village elder told them he expected more money. He also complained about the constant gunfire in the valley. Explosions and rifle fire were continuously going off in the valley around the encampment and he worried for the lives of his villagers. He left unhappy.

The ETTs were surprised to hear a helicopter in the distance. Looking up, they could see a Russian HIND flying in. It landed near Kamdesh.

"It must be here to get the ballots," Assumed Longfield.

Not much later, the HIND took off and headed back for Kabul. Everyone was glad to know the elections had been successful, but they couldn't help but still wonder why they couldn't get air assets from US, Coalition, or Afghan forces when Afghan government helicopters were flying in.

It was later in the day now, toward dusk, and one of the ANA approached Oles with some trash. It was obvious what he was hinting at.

"Collect the trash," said Oles. Actually, he had been looking forward to this ritual as much as the ANA. It was the only thing to do other than play cards. Oles walked out of the CP and saw the ANA hanging around in anticipation. Almost forty men were spread out around the two buildings, watching. By now some of the villagers had heard of the nightly ceremony, too, because several of them appeared downstream to sit on the rocks, patiently waiting for the flaming raft to pass before them. Apparently, word had spread how these crazy Americans sent a burning boat down the river every night.

The ANA eagerly collected trash from the compound and placed it on the raft. Oles dowsed it with kerosene, lit it, and pushed it into the river. He noticed several of the ANA again laughing hysterically. It made Oles laugh, also. As before, the ANA ran down to the water's edge and watched as the river swept the flaming barge downstream. Some were cheering as they watched the box disappear around the bend in the river. It was the only activity that seemed to revive their flagging morale.

Dawson, like the ANA, always got a big kick out of their nightly arson. It was funny to watch the burning raft float majestically down the river in the midst of the worst situation Dawson had ever been in. But what was even funnier was to watch the reaction of the ANA soldiers. They absolutely loved the nightly raft burning. They all dropped whatever boring task they were doing or paying attention to and watched the naval arson. Dawson took great pride in the fact that he had started it. He also thought it was hilarious that Oles kept it going. Dawson thought he and Oles had similar psyches. To Dawson, Oles was a great officer. He wasn't the type to consider his career and personal interests above his mission or his soldiers. Dawson felt you could bank on whatever Oles said.

He remembered the first time he met Oles. They were in Bosnia at a "March Madness Meeting" for their unit. The HQ staff was feeding everyone what Dawson called "the typical kool-aid crap". Dawson hated it so much he slipped out to…*go to the bathroom*. He was standing in the lobby killing time when he heard a voice from behind him say, "This is bullshit! Uniform welfare!" Dawson turned and met Captain Marc Oles for the first time. Oles had *gone to the bathroom,* too. The two stood in the lobby and talked about home and life stateside.

It was now dusk, almost two years later, and Oles and Dawson went back for Oles's nightly call to BDE HQ. He wondered if they finally had something for him. Since their battlegroup was leaving Kamdesh tomorrow, a plan for their departure seemed reasonable.

The Americans could hear the Muslims praying. Although the ANA insisted the people of Kamdesh were not Muslim, at least some of the villagers incorporated Muslim prayers because they could be heard praying and chanting several times a day and at least once in the middle of the night. The Afghan Police and ANA completed their daily prayers throughout the mission, but there were no mosques for them to attend. They said their prayers together in a large group, spread out on their hands and knees on their mats, facing Mecca, leaning forward with heads to the ground in supplication. One person would recite the prayers and the rest would follow the traditional rituals. The ANA were gathered together in the compound doing just that as Oles picked up the radio to call BDE.

"Come in, Saber 3."

Nothing. Oles tried again but he couldn't raise BDE. They discovered their radio had problems. It seemed to be working because they could occasionally hear other conversations; however, they could not send. Since Midwest had a cell phone, Oles passed word for him to call BDE and tell them to call him. Midwest made the call and within minutes Saber 3 was on the radio.

"Come in (Omega 6). How's it going up there?"

After giving BDE his SITREP, Oles asked, "What is the status on our comprehensive extraction plan?"

"Be advised, we are still formulating said plan." Then Oles heard Saber 3's tone change. *"(Omega 6), I received a call from one of your sergeants."* The colonel went on to explain that Midwest had called him and told him how bad things were. He reminded Oles how important it was too keep him off any unsecured phone lines and to maintain radio discipline and keep him off the command net.

"Yes, sir."

Oles signed off from BDE and called the SF. He called them every night, and they talked and laughed about the ridiculousness of the situation. The first thing they mentioned was Midwest. The SF had gotten a big kick out of the frightened sergeant's radio call to BDE. They were laughing and told Oles it was some of the best entertainment they had. Oles couldn't help but snicker because it was funny. Oles knew it was guys like Midwest who gave the National Guard a bad reputation among the other branches of the armed forces. When they finished talking, Oles got off the radio and went to find Midwest. "Hey," he said, trying to be patient, "you gotta stay off the radio. The colonel's getting pissed."

WASHINGTON, D.C.

Although Sept. 20, 2005, had come and gone on the Asian continent, the day was just dawning in the United States. Defense Secretary Donald Rumsfeld began a news briefing at the Pentagon:

"The successful parliamentary elections in Afghanistan Sept. 18 have proven wrong all critics of U.S. efforts in that country." He continued. "Critics of the war in Afghanistan were not just wrong, they were harmful because they made the cause seem hopeless," Rumsfeld added, "The millions of Afghan citizens who turned out to vote proved them wrong, and terrorists weren't able to affect the elections."[13]

"After the IED I wanted to go to Mandagal and get into a fight. I was just pissed off. We couldn't, we didn't have medical supplies and I knew medevac would be iffy at best. That and we didn't have enough men. Remember, a few of the ANA just took off their uniforms and turned in their weapons and quit the Army because they thought we were fucked."

Captain Marc Oles

RELOCATE
September 21

Oles awoke at dawn. He was in a good mood. They were leaving Kamdesh today. As he always did, he stepped outside to check their compound.

"Crack!"

The distant report of an AK echoed down the mountainous canyon. From the sound of the weapon, Oles could tell it was very far away. He couldn't even see the shooter.

"Is some asshole just trying to piss me off?" he thought.

"Crack!" went the report again. This time Oles marked the shooter. The man was up in the same distant cliffs, between 900 and 1,000 meters away. He was firing with an AK. The guy was aiming at him, that was certain, but Oles couldn't even hear the bullets' impact. More often than not, ACM snipers would try to engage their targets from a range completely unrealistic for their weapon. Oles felt they did this because they didn't want to be close enough to receive effective return fire. Oles went about his business checking their O-Ps. Then he went back to his Ford to call BDE.

"Saber 3, what is the status on the comprehensive plan for today's extraction?" Oles assumed Saber 3 would have nothing for them. He was certain that just as they had advanced into Kamdesh on their own, they would have to withdraw on their own. He asked again because he was bored and liked to needle BDE. Oles was unprepared for what Saber 3 had to say to him. BDE told him they could not leave today and advised him they needed to remain another twenty-four hours. He was told it was vital to the national elections that they remain in Kamdesh an additional day. Oles got off the radio, wondering how he would break the bad news to his ETTs. He didn't need to. They had all been listening.

Longfield was used to bad news in the Army. It was like the sunrise. It came daily. But the situation was wearing on him, nonetheless. Dawson and Strate received the information in a similar, resigned manner. Midwest did not take the news well at all.

The daily patrol went out. As usual, the soldiers proceeded 1,000 meters in each direction. One IED was found. It was destroyed and the patrol returned without incident.

Since their arrival locals would visit, promise their support, and then disappear. Later some would come back and pretend they had pledged nothing. The Americans wondered if they were sizing the place up and taking mental notes to give to the bad guys because when the locals left, they would immediately get on their cell phones. The ETTs would watch them as they walked away. Several of them arrived at the compound again.

Because of the visits and because the shooters seemed to be in multiple locations around their camp, Oles gave the order to move their position in order to bring a temporary reprieve to the harassing fire and possibly thwart an impeding attack. He had an additional reason, too. Their old outhouse had been used by seventy men for almost a week; it was full of human waste and stunk unbearably. It had also attracted seemingly hundreds of flies. There was a dire need for another latrine to allow someplace for the soldiers to relive themselves without a fearful spread of dysentery. A new camp would solve that problem as well.

They headed to a spot about 10 kilometers from their old position. It was closer but not quite to Kamdesh. The good news was that it was further from Mandagal. They didn't take much fire while they loaded their vehicles, and the ETTs wondered if this was because the ACM thought they were leaving for good. It might have appeared that way to anybody watching as they broke camp and loaded their trucks. Using their metal detectors, the column of vehicles slowly crawled along the Nuristan Road toward Kamdesh. They arrived almost two hours later and began to break camp.

Their new position consisted of a building with a walled area suitable for a compound, but they didn't have an outhouse. They needed one close enough for safety but far enough away not to stink and attract flies. Dawson and Strate were told to check out a dilapidated building just down the road as a possible latrine. Followed by a squad of ANA, they moved over to the structure. They had passed it on the way in, but it had been too dark to see clearly. The building was decrepit with no roof and only three sides. It was constructed of football-sized rocks like most of the structures in the country but the walls were only about shoulder high, perhaps five feet. Dawson and Strate approached the door. It was obvious even before they entered that the interior of the structure was overgrown with vegetation.

Dawson's eyebrows rose when he saw the plants.

Beside him he heard Strate say, "You know what that is, don't you?"

"Weed."

"Yeah," laughed Strate, "that's weed!"

Dawson almost started laughing. He didn't smoke marijuana, but the situation just seemed to fit with this mission. They were told to find a latrine and what do they discover? Marijuana! Dawson didn't even have time to think of something ironic to say before Strate went to work chopping down the tall plants. Strate was laughing as he slashed away.

Soon Strate had most of the room cleared and a huge pile of Marijuana stacked in the corner of the hut. They discussed what to do with the marijuana and considered leaving it there.

"Let's burn it!" said Dawson. He knew the ANA loved to burn things, and the last thing he wanted to do was move it himself.

"Yeah," laughed Strate, "it will be incense for the new latrine."

Snickering, the two lit the freshly-cut green-leaf plants. Soon, a large plume of smoke was wafting into the sky. They returned to the compound and were promptly asked by the others what all the smoke was about. Everyone laughed when they were told about the marijuana. It just seemed to fit the mission.

Strate was approached by the LTC. His company was running out of rations and needed to purchase food from Kamdesh. Strate knew this was true and doled out $50,000 Afghani. The ANA sent a patrol to Kamdesh to buy rice, potatoes, and goat meat.

Simultaneously, Dawson was approached by Rahim. The ANA CPT said he, too, needed money for food for his Kandak. Dawson gave him $20,000 Afghani for supplies. Only when they got back, Rahim said he had not been given enough money and demanded more. Dawson refused. Then the LTC from Strate's Kandak reported that Rahim only used $5,000 Afghani of his allotted money to buy food for his troops and kept the rest. Dawson was furious and approached Oles about it. Oles told him to remain calm and keep records of everything that was going on. This was neither the time nor the place to have infighting.

Bored, and with little to do, the ETTs again decided to play cards. Strate, Dawson, and Midwest were already inside sitting down to play but they needed a forth. Dawson went to get Longfield.

"Hey, how about a game of cards?"

"I ain't playing with that fuckin' guy," said Longfield, referring to Midwest. "That son-of-a-bitch is a cheater."

"Come on, everybody knows he's a cheater. He sucks, anyway."

Longfield thought about it. Then he said, "Okay. I'll play. But I'm not on that son-of-a-bitch's team." Longfield went in and sat down. By now everyone knew Midwest cheated, but he was not very good at cards so nobody cared. They didn't even watch him closely anymore.

The day passed with the ANA constantly firing their weapons. It was always return fire, a burst of PKM or AK fire up at the shooters on the ridge, but it had become so frequent it was no longer alarming—only loud.

There was one new development. Since the medicine arrival, the ANA were constantly coming in and asking for pills. Rahim was one of the first to ask. He claimed to be sick and in need of medication. Oles told him they couldn't give out any medicine. The ANA CPT left angry. After a half dozen more ANA came in asking for medicine, Oles began to get frustrated. The medicine labels were not in English. None of the Americans even knew what they were. It seemed to Dawson and Longfield, unless you had gone to medical school or had some sort of medical training, you couldn't identify anything by reading the labels. Some of the only meds they recognized were marked "Laxative" and "Stool softener."

Another ANA soldier arrived in the CP.

"What do you fuckin' want?" groaned Oles.

The ANA soldier pointed at the medicine box.

"If I give you that, it could fuckin' kill you!"

The ANA soldier got annoyed and left. Shortly thereafter, the Terp arrived with several ANA in tow. He asked for pills and claimed the soldiers with him were not feeling well.

"Look," said Oles," before this medicine showed up, nobody was sick. Now everybody is sick and needs medicine. No! We're not giving out medicine."

Then Rahim arrived again. He demanded drugs for his headache and said he wouldn't leave until he got some.

"Here," said Oles, handing Rahim a laxative, "this will fix your headache."

Maybe an hour later, Rahim came back into the CP. He still claimed to have a headache. Oles reached into the box, took another laxative and handed it over. Rahim left.

"Collect the trash!"

Dusk was setting on the fifth day. From their new position Oles sent another flaming raft down the river. Oles continually marveled at how the ANA never grew tired of the raft-burning. It was the one singular event that made them happy. By now most of Kamdesh had heard about the burning rafts and several more villagers turned out to watch. They could be seen only briefly, shadows appearing in the coming dusk. The Americans could almost see why they came. There didn't seem to be anything to do in Nuristan. Oles wondered if it was a morale event for the Taliban and ACM as well. Maybe they, too, were up in the cliffs waiting for his nightly raft to pass flaming beneath them.

Oles called his sergeants together for their daily briefing. As usual, everyone talked about being pleasantly surprised that they hadn't been hit that day because everyone expected it. As the direction of the conversation often went, the discussion was about what to do should they get attacked. Oles and the others loved this part of the talk because Midwest hated it so much. At the very mention of what to do with their dead bodies, he grimaced and tried to change the subject to something more positive—like their extraction. The others got such a kick out of how upset Midwest got, it made them talk more openly of their impending doom.

"How do you think we're going to die?"

"Do you think they'll ever find our beheaded corpses?"

At each of these questions Oles watched Midwest grow paler. Oles went to his truck to call BDE.

"Saber 3. This is (Omega 6). Come in, over."

"*This is Saber 5. We read you, (Omega 6).*"

"Saber 5, what is the status on the comprehensive extraction plan?" By now it was a running joke. Oles deliberately asked the same question every night just to hear HQ stammer at their own inability to answer. However, tonight Saber 5 was on the radio. Saber 5 was new to the conversations, so they probably didn't get Oles's sarcasm.

"*Be advised*," said Saber 5, "*we are still formulating that plan.*" Oles gave the officer a SITREP and listened as he was fed more and more of what Oles called "bullshit". Only this time, Saber 5, the BDE XO, was feeding Oles more "bullshit" than he could stomach. Finally, in frustration Oles said, "Saber 5, is Saber 3 or Saber 4 in the CP?"

Pause.

"*Ahhh...Affirmative, hold for Saber 3.*"

FOB NARAY

The SF operatives at Naray were howling with laughter. Some were listening in their CP, but two were down near the border listening in their truck. They were all cracking up. What that National Guard CPT had said was polite enough, but to anyone in the military, by asking Saber 5 if Saber 3 or Saber 4 was available, the officer may as well have said, "You are a fucking idiot. Give me someone with a brain." The SF had been listening to the Americans in Nuristan for several days now and actually looked forward to their nightly radio calls. They were hilarious and the SF never missed them. The National Guard captain in charge of the ANA detachment was steadily getting more and more "shitty" with his colonel back at HQ with every "spoon-full of bullshit" they tried to feed him. The SF had begun to think of the situation like it was a crazy sitcom.

KAMDESH

"This is Saber 3," squawked the radio. *"Listen, (Omega 6). We are still working out your extraction plan. Be patient."* Then Saber 3 said, *"I received another call from your sergeant today. Please keep that individual off the command net. Over."*

"Roger that, Saber 3. (Omega 6) out."

Oles got off the radio and turned to Midwest. "Hey, stay off the damn radio. Stop calling them." Oles rarely got mad but he was becoming increasingly irritated with Midwest. Oles then picked up the radio and called the SF. They were laughing when they answered. The calls from Midwest back to BDE were too much, and the conversation with Saber 5 had them howling. The way they laughed when they repeated the conversation to Oles made him snicker.

TUESDAY SEPTEMBER 20 2005

Had a Sgt & a Lt get into a scuffle over food which escalated to a gun being grabbed.

Higher has decided we need to stay put for at least 2 days til they can gin up an ealop order for our return. We think this is now an exercise for MOD to practice, an attempt to control our malice and basically higher thumbing their nose at us. The ballots leave tonight, but we're being told to stay until maybe the 25th. The money is flowing like water now - with receipts just being signed by the CO. If we did that with Op funds we'd be in jail. At least Childress sent a resupply. The local who promised support took 50K, a box of meds and said he wants more. Oles is done paying looks like we're hoping for the best on the way out.

WEDNESDAY SEPTEMBER 21 2005

Moved about 10km closer to home but still not in Kandesh. We gave out 50K(A) to Kandak 32 for food and found out weapons had only used 5K of theirs. We're awaiting the order to move out but only have 80K(A) left. The Wpns CO is irritating everybody with his pestering and weaseling for money. Oles wants to puch im, now he seems to think the house rental was 50K... Brilliant use of the US wallet.

SSG Dawson's journal entries for September 20-21

A view of the compound from the side of the river

The nightly morale event—Oles's flaming raft is set afire and set adrift.

"Captain Oles is a stand up guy. He will tell you what's on his mind. If you don't like it, he don't care. (He) won't hold nothin' back. Captain Oles is the best officer I ever served under."

Staff Sergeant Scott Strate

SURROUNDED
September 22

The ETTs woke to simultaneous rifle fire from the northeast and the southwest ridges. As usual, it was too far away to be effective, but it showed they were surrounded. The ANA blasted back up at the cliffs, wasting ammunition. The firing went on all morning. Occasionally, RPGs were discharged by both sides. They always landed well short of their targets, but their explosions echoed down the valley.

The ANA were increasingly uneasy and their morale was dangerously low. The ETTs also were suffering low morale. Oles had called back to brigade for orders on their extraction but just learned from Saber 3 that they were to stay in Kamdesh another twenty-four hours.

Dawson, Strate, Longfield, Midwest, and Oles sat or stood in the CP talking among themselves. Questions were being asked, but no one was expecting any answers; they were just venting aloud. [14]

"When are we leaving this hellhole?" voiced Dawson.

"Why the hell are we here?" said Strate. "We haven't had any effect on the elections one way or the other."

"Right! You're right!" agreed Midwest. "And we were supposed to leave yesterday. So let's get out of here. Let's leave."

"And what good has our presence here done anyway?"

"We haven't gone further than a thousand meters from our compound since we arrived."

"No shit."

"So, let's go!" urged Midwest. "Let's go now!"

"It's our mission," said Longfield. "We are at the mercy of the commanders. We've got to finish the mission. We can sit and bitch, but we still got to do it. We've got to figure out how to do it and get out of here alive." It wasn't that Longfield didn't agree with what the others were saying, but he felt someone had to be positive or their morale would plunge even more.

Throughout their many bitching sessions, Oles only listened as his sergeants vented in frustration. At any other time, in almost any other situation, he would have said something positive to keep the morale of his soldiers in a better state. However, Oles had been given so much "cool-aid crap" from higher HQ that he didn't have the heart to "bullshit" his own men. Things were the way they were and that was that.

"We gotta get out of here!" insisted Midwest. "We gotta just load up the trucks and get out of here!"

"The whole chain of command let us down," said Dawson.

"Every last one of them," said Strate.

Oles didn't say anything but he agreed with Strate and Dawson on that one. Everyone had let them down. Every last officer he had contacted or spoken with at BDE HQ failed in every respect to get their soldiers any of the orders or backup that was SOP for an operation in the field. As Oles listened to his sergeants, he couldn't help but feel bad for them. Being stuck in one of the most remote, primitive, and dangerous corners of the world was probably not what any of them had in mind when they joined the Guard. Still, listening to Midwest sometimes tested his patience. The guy was an E-7. He should know better.

"You know," said Longfield, "it's very possible that they don't have any fuckin' control over this. They were probably told to send us. This is political. This is bigger than the Army."

To that everyone agreed. The American soldiers in Kamdesh felt the orders for this operation had come from outside the military.

Dawson thought about Longfield's theory. Although he agreed with it, he thought Longfield was too idealistic. He liked Longfield but, in his opinion, the sergeant was too quick to always defend the Army. He knew Longfield wasn't a kool-aid drinker, though. In fact, back at

Asadabad before the mission, everyone had heard that Longfield got in trouble for telling some "Hesco Hobbit" of a colonel that he wasn't doing his job. That was apparently why he was out in Asadabad in the first place. It had been a form of disciplinary action on the part of the colonel and a way of getting rid of the NCO who was exposing him for being a slacker.

Longfield, for his part, thought Dawson was not military enough although he knew Dawson was a very good soldier. Longfield felt Dawson was way too skeptical of everything that came from higher. He knew Dawson (at times) had reason to feel that way, but sometimes a soldier had to shut up and follow orders. It was like Tennyson said in his famous *Charge of the Light Brigade*, "Theirs not to make reply, theirs not to reason why, theirs but to do and die." As much as a soldier might hate doing what was ordered, it was part of being a soldier.

Even though Longfield felt Dawson was cynical and skeptical, he also thought the red-head was one of the most likeable guys he knew and felt he was as loyal as any soldier in the field. Given an order in combat, Dawson would obey every one.

The discussion ended and Oles ordered the daily patrol to head out. The patrol, as usual, traveled 1,000 meters down the road in both directions. Whichever direction the patrol headed first, the gunfire stopped in that area. When the patrol backtracked and went the other way, the gunfire resumed. One IED was picked up. There were no casualties.

Word passed to the ETTs from the Kandak 34 commander that the ANA had their own orders to leave the following day. That was good news. Of course, it had to be verified by TFP, but everyone hoped the news would be confirmed when they spoke to BDE.

Dawson was walking through the compound checking on his soldiers when he saw the ANA captain. He did a double-take. The ANA officer was wearing what the Americans called "a man dress"— meaning he was wearing typical Afghan garb.

"Why isn't he in his ANA officer's uniform," thought Dawson. The sergeant's immediate thought was to go warn the others. Everyone suspected the ANA captain played for both sides. The Americans had been told the man's family bought his position in the Army. His family had made an investment in his future and, from what the ETTs heard, that occurrence was not uncommon. Dawson felt this man being in local dress meant nothing good. However, nobody else seemed to be bothered by it. None of the ETTs had said anything, and the ANA appeared completely unconcerned. Dawson fought the urge to talk to Oles about it. For one, he knew Oles had to have already seen the man, and he hadn't mentioned it. Two, Dawson knew everybody was already on edge. He didn't want to make their situation any worse. If the ANA Captain had their betrayal to the Taliban or ACM in mind, they would all find out soon enough.

"Why is someone burning an ANA uniform?" Dawson heard Longfield ask.

Dawson looked over and saw a small fire with what looked like an ANA uniform burning atop it. The ETTs had a Terp repeat the question to the ANA soldier who was burning the uniform. The man responded and the Terp turned and explained. The uniform was the ANA Captain's. Apparently, he had defecated on himself. He made one of his soldiers get rid of it.

A light bulb went off in Dawson's head. He felt like laughing. It now seemed obvious why the ANA captain was wearing the man-dress. He had taken two laxatives the day before. He had obviously soiled himself. It was the one bright moment of Dawson's day.

The hours passed with the compound taking random gunfire and the men waiting to be hit by several hundred attackers. So far, only a few dozen seemed to be cracking off shots at them from the ridgeline.

Every two or three hours the ETTs and their ANA counterparts watched an old vehicle or a few pedestrians approach, but there was little traffic. The Afghan police would stop by at least once a day and pass information to the ANA. The Americans noticed (and had since their arrival) there was no love lost between the ANP and the ANA. They were reluctant, distrustful allies.

No one talked about it, but there was an undeclared three-way power-struggle in the Kamdesh area. The local elders wanted to maintain their control and resented the ANA presence (which represented the new government). However, they knew resistance of any kind toward the ANA might bring more troops from Kabul (along with American firepower). By subtle cooperation the local elders hoped the ANA would leave soon, and things would return to normal.

At the same time they did not want to appear to be collaborating with the ANA/Americans. That would undoubtedly cause trouble with their neighboring Pakistanis or the ACM/Taliban/al-Qaeda they harbored, who were only a few miles away. Any cooperation with the new government might create a blood feud after the ANA left. The local elders were trying to avoid both of those possibilities and simply wanted to keep the peace.

The ACM/Taliban/al-Qaeda in the area were just across the border in Pakistan, under the protection of an anti-American warlord. No one knew what had kept the four hundred ACM from hitting the ANA compound, but it was suspected it was a combination of several concerns—American retaliation, an increased, permanent ANA (and American) presence, and a blood feud with the local villagers of the Kamdesh/Nuristan area. Since their own local intel reported the US and ANA were leaving soon, they were probably content to let them leave without stirring up trouble and making them come back in strength.

Lastly, the ANA, representing the new government, were the third force in the region. They attempted a brave show of force but were obviously the weaklings on the block. Luckily the other two factions didn't seem to know that yet. So far, all three groups were afraid of escalation.

The day ended with the incessant gunfire from the cliffs stopping just before Oles burned their nightly raft.

"Saber 3, what is the status on our comprehensive plan?"

"*Be advised, we are formulating that plan and will get back to you ASAP.*" Then Saber 3 became angry and told Oles about Midwest's latest radio call back to BDE HQ earlier that day. "*You gotta keep that asshole off the radio. You've gotta calm him down.*"

"Roger, sir," replied Oles. "I will talk to that individual." Oles was just as frustrated. As if he didn't have enough on his plate, Midwest kept calling the BDE commander to tell him how bad things were up in Kamdesh. Oles inwardly hoped they would get so sick of Midwest that they would fly someone in to relieve him. However, realistically, he knew that wasn't going to happen. He also knew there was no way anyone was going to come and get them. Oles knew if he and his men were going to get out, it would be by themselves, with nothing but verbal orders from above and no help.

"Hey!" he called to Midwest, "Stop calling BDE! They're getting pissed! That's an order!"

What the colonel hadn't explained to Oles was that Midwest wasn't just using the radio. He was making calls back on his own unsecured cell phone. That was part of the problem.

It was late now, around 2300. Longfield was manning the checkpoint outside their CP. His Terp was standing outside the compound wall talking to some of his fellow ANA soldiers. A vehicle pulled up with six men in it. Longfield thought something was fishy. Cars didn't usually drive at night in Nuristan, so something was not quite right. Even though a few vehicles passed back and forth during the day, traffic usually stopped by dusk. In addition, the vehicle had come from either Mandagal or out of Pakistan, Longfield noted. However, the ANA did not seem alarmed. They began talking to the men in the vehicle.

Longfield listened to the conversation as well as he could, but it was no use. They were speaking too fast, and they used a dialect he was completely unfamiliar with. He could catch almost nothing of the conversation. Then Longfield's Terp walked over to him casually and said, "I asked them, 'What are you doing here? Why are you driving down this road?' The driver said, 'We're Afghan Police. Let us through.' Then he handed me this." The Terp handed Longfield a card and a piece of paper. Longfield looked at both and saw what appeared to be Arabic script. He had no idea what either one was or said.

"What is it? What's it say?"

"It's a student card from a college in Pakistan and a letter from a father to his son."

Longfield knew instantly the driver was trying to bluff his way through. So many of the ANA were illiterate, this driver probably figured he could fake his way past. If none of the ANA could read, they probably would believe him. Luckily, this Terp could read. Longfield could tell the ANA nearby were suddenly scared. Most of them were always frightened, but the checkpoint guards were clearly uneasy. Longfield took the card and the letter and showed them to the LTC, saying, "Look at this shit." The ANA commander looked it over and had some of his men go back to the vehicle. Longfield was able to catch a little of what was being said.

"This is bullshit," said an ANA sergeant to the driver. Longfield understood that message. By now he was fluent in most of the curse words. The driver knew he was busted and suddenly changed his story. Longfield's Terp spoke beside him, "They keep breaking into different languages. They are speaking Pashto, Urdu, and Dari."

The ANA sergeant came back and talked to the LTC. Longfield knew they had caught the suspicious-looking men in the car lying straight up. But the colonel turned to Longfield and said, "We can't do anything with them here. We don't have anywhere to hold them."

"Contact some local police," said Longfield. "Have some local police come up and let them do their job. They have a lot more guys than we do and cells to hold these guys in."

The LTC went out and questioned the men himself. Then he walked back in.

"So what are we doing?" asked Longfield.

"I let them go." Just as the colonel spoke, the vehicle started up.

"*What*?" Longfield couldn't believe this was happening. The vehicle started to drive away. The LTC, obviously noting Longfield's anger, spoke to Longfield's Terp for translation.

"We know there are ACM in the area. We are going to let them go because if we don't, we are going to have problems. With the ACM all over these mountains, even if we had more ANA here, it wouldn't be enough. We will get our asses shot because they will be pissed off at us for taking their men."

Longfield was furious. He hated to admit that the LTC's decision was the right one; and realizing that fact was almost worse. Longfield knew they were leaving tomorrow and the last thing they wanted to do was piss anyone off. They'd been lucky since the day of the IED blast. The last thing they needed now was to make the men who had them surrounded angrier.

"This is a fucked up way to look at it," thought Longfield, "but he has a point."

"Remember the BDE answer that a 'comprehensive plan' was being conceived to extract us? It became a running joke and when I would call them I would ask if they had the 'comprehensive plan' completed. It never happened. The SF were the only ones that seemed to really give a shit. They constantly provided us info and intel—like the call of "jihad" against the infidels in Kamdesh by the tribal chief in Pakistan. We were the only infidels in Nuristan. There were hundreds of dudes coming across the boarder to slaughter us."

Captain Marc Oles

INFIGHTING
September 23

With the mission appearing to be on its last day and AK fire still echoing off the ridges, the Weapons Company CO approached Dawson in front of a number of his ANA soldiers. He handed over a few receipts and asked Dawson for the money. Making sure he spoke loud enough for his soldiers to hear, Rahim also told Dawson any leftover money should be distributed among the soldiers as a bonus. Dawson almost laughed at that, but he held such a dislike for Rahim, he simply said, "NO!"

Right at that moment, one of the locals showed up at their compound and demanded money. He claimed the ANA had ruined his crops for the year. The man said he would not be able to make it through the winter now and demanded compensation. He wanted $30,000 Afghani ($800 US). Dawson refused to pay so much and began haggling with the man. They came to terms on a reduced price. Rahim went purple with rage when Dawson paid the man for the damaged crops.

Rahim was so livid about the money issues he immediately told his ANA soldiers that the Americans were squandering their bonus money. The ANA, in turn, became furious and appeared to be starting another revolt. Longfield was confronted before he could reenter the compound. His Terp spoke in rapid fire, telling him what the furious ANA were saying.

"Why did you pay so much for the field?"

"We should take it for free!"

Everyone was talking and shouting angrily in broken English, Dari, or Posto.

Dawson seethed. "This is all because of the Weapons CO," he thought to himself.

The ANA were enraged. Dawson and Longfield tried to calm them down but they were so irate at what their commander had told them that they were almost beyond reason. The ANA LTC came over and tried to calm the Afghan solders down, but even he couldn't do it. He and Rahim came to words and began shouting at each other.

Oles came over to see what the infighting was about and, for the first time, actually got mad at Dawson and Longfield. He knew the Weapons CO was at the heart of the problem, but he was upset that the friction had occurred in the first place.

Dawson and Longfield, for their part, hadn't done anything wrong and were irritated at their CO's rebuke. The stress of the situation was wearing on everyone. When Rahim approached Dawson and told him the money Nasir stole should be divided among the troops as a "gift," Dawson could barely control his anger. "No," he said as he moved away.

Dawson went over to talk to Oles. He knew his CO was unhappy with the infighting, but he wanted him to know neither he nor Longfield had started it. Oles knew. He was just frustrated. Dawson explained how Rahim had stolen thousands of US tax paying Dollars and was still trying to pilfer more with bogus receipts. He suggested to Oles that they place him under arrest right now.

Oles wouldn't have minded doing that. In fact, he wanted to. They certainly had enough evidence as far as he was concerned. But he wondered how much civil war the arrest would bring among the ANA. Either the two ANA companies would fight against each other, or they would band together against the Americans. Either way, it was a lose-lose situation for the ETTs, and they still had the ACM and Taliban to worry about. They needed every weapon they could bring to bear if they were to get out of Kamdesh alive.

Then came the same bad news they had received for the last few days. Brigade was ordering them to stay in Nuristan an additional day. When Oles spread the news, the ANA morale hit rock bottom; the ETT morale was not much better. AK fire continued right up until sunset, stopping only evidently for Oles's nightly raft burning.

Pentagon, Washington, D.C.

President George W. Bush made the following announcement from the Pentagon:

"The successful September 18 elections in Afghanistan signify a vital step toward democracy in that country, and the situation there is an example of the progress being made in the war on terror." President Bush continued, "Afghanistan is still a work in progress, and nearly 18,000 U.S. troops are still there serving as part of the coalition. There are still terrorists who want to overthrow the new Afghan government, and the U.S. and the international community are dedicated to thwarting their attempts."[15]

THURSDAY SEPTEMBER 2005 22

K32 commander got a call from MOD saying we'll get orders to move tomorrow. Guess the comprehensive plan is all for naught. Looks like the U3 has gotten us an Anti IED burn run but we have to now wait until the 25th. They can't resupply us but Childress sent us enough MRE & water to probably make it.
Everybody but me is eaten up by mites. Hammer looks like he's got chickenpox, poor kid.

FRIDAY SEPTEMBER 2005 23

Another glorious day. WpnsCo has started to be a complete idiot by telling his troops that whatever money is left over is their bonus. When the local farmer came to ask for pay - his crops were damaged by ANA - there was a near riot and Oles got honked off at me & Longfield. Whatever, all the heartburn is coming directly from WpnsCO & the BC of Kandak 32 is disgusted but can't rein Wpns in. WpnsCO suggested we split up the $ Nasir stole and give it to the troops as a "gift". I'd like to cuff him right now but Oles keeps reminding us we need every gun. WpnCo is playing all sides against us and I'm tired of it.

SSG Dawson's journal entries for September 22 and 23

"That last night I was so frustrated I told BDE we would attack east and get ourselves out. The SF told us to expect several contacts on the way. I didn't care. I just wanted it over with one way or the other."

Captain Marc Oles

REBELLION IN THE ANA
September 24

"Saber 3, what is the status on the comprehensive plan for our extraction?" Oles didn't show it but he was inwardly concerned BDE would keep them in Kamdesh another day. He didn't know how he'd be able to keep up morale if HQ postponed their extraction yet again.

"(Omega 6), what are your uniform sizes?"

"Uniform sizes?" asked Oles. Longfield was nearby, also listening. He was just as startled. Midwest had a look of such horror on his face that Oles almost laughed.

"*Affirmative,*" said Saber 3. "*We need to know your sizes to send you winter clothing. We're going to keep you guys there for another forty-five days.*"

It was as if everyone had just learned of the death of a family member. Saber 3 continued, "You have to stay forty-five days after the elections and secure it." BDE gave the Guardsmen nothing more, just orders to stay. Longfield happened to glance over at Midwest, and the look of unbridled terror on the sergeant's face helped ease his rising anger.

"Roger that," said Oles sullenly, "will get our uniform sizes to you. Out."

Oles got off the radio and felt like banging his head against the Ford Ranger. He was about to swear in frustration when Midwest cracked from the stain.

"WE CAN'T STAY HERE ANOTHER FORTY-FIVE DAYS!" shrieked the stocky Midwesterner. "WE GOTTA LOAD UP THE TRUCK AND GET THE HELL OUT OF HERE!"

"You can't just load up the truck and leave," said Longfield bitterly. He was sick and tired of Midwest's lack of self-control. "You've been ordered to stay here. We gotta stay here."

"NO, WE GOTTA GET OUT OF HERE!" Midwest was panicking. "WE JUST WON'T TELL ANYBODY! WE'LL JUST SHOW UP!"

Longfield looked at Midwest in astonishment. So did Oles and Dawson. The outburst didn't surprise Strate at all.

"You must have missed the fuckin' day they taught Army at Army school," said Longfield.

"Are you fuckin' scared of everything?" said Oles to the sergeant. Oles, too, had had enough of Midwest, who now looked like he was going to cry.

Longfield was astounded that an American soldier could act this way. "Holy shit, dude," he said in amazement, "you're in the Army."

Oles was as frustrated as he'd ever been. This whole mission stank to high heaven and had from day one. No written orders, no support, daily IEDs, two KIA's, multiple wounded with two amputees, problems with the ANA—the list went on. They were originally only supposed to stay in Kamdesh for five days. Now, on day seven, they were told they would stay another forty-five days. They had already run out of water and were down to their last MREs. Oles snickered at the thought that they wouldn't even have enough trash to make a raft to burn tomorrow because they were running out of supplies. But it was out of Oles's hands. In frustration he passed the word to his Terp and told him to let the LTC know his soldiers would remain in Nuristan for another month and a half.

The Terp spoke to the ANA commander, and Oles could understand what he was saying because his Posto was better with each day and he already knew the message. The Terp didn't even finish his sentence before the LTC exploded. The expletives erupted from his mouth. He became so irate he stormed over to his radio and called higher ANA HQ. Oles tried to listen but the LTC was talking so fast it was difficult for Oles to understand. Still, he was able to gather most of the conversation.

"WE ARE LEAVING ON SEPTEMBER TWENTY-FIFTH!" roared the LTC. After a short pause, he spat, "NO! WE ARE LEAVING!" Another pause was followed by a furious, "I DON'T GIVE A SHIT! WE ARE LEAVING ON SEPTEMBER TWENTY-FIFTH!"

The LTC slammed down the receiver and stormed out. Not more than two minutes later Oles received a radio call from his own BDE HQ.

"The ANA are not to leave. They are needed to stay and secure the elections. You are to keep them there."

"How are we going to keep them here?" asked Oles.

Pause.

Not having an answer, the reply was, *"If they leave, it's your ass."* Military formality had long since dropped from their radio calls.

"What if we can't stop them?" said Oles incredulously. He didn't "give a shit" about his career anymore; it was his life he was worried about. "What do we do? You know there are over fifty ANA and only five Americans, don't you?"

Pause.

There was no answer from the other end until a repeated, *"The ANA are not to leave. You have your orders. Saber 3, out."*

Oles got off the radio and motioned for his Terp to follow him. He went over to the LTC. The furious ANA commander had already told his soldiers they were leaving. The ANA looked as though they were finally experiencing good morale. They were policing their bivouac and getting things ready to be loaded into the trucks.

"Translate for me," said Oles to his Terp.

"We have orders to stay. We Americans are staying." This was a gamble. Oles knew the LTC had been ordered to remain with the Americans. The Afghan commander looked darkly at Oles. He was absolutely seething with rage. He knew if the Americans stayed, he had to as well.

"YOU ARE FOOLS!" shouted the LTC. "THEY WILL KILL YOU ALL! AS IT IS YOU ARE LUCKY YOU ARE STILL ALIVE!"

"Those are our orders," replied Oles calmly. "There's nothing we can do." Even though the LTC was the more cooperative of the two senior ANA officers, Oles was so used to the man being irate, it didn't even bother him anymore.

In an absolute rage, the LTC whirled around and shouted at his men to stop their packing. He roared at them to put their equipment and belongings back, explaining that they were staying because (pointing at Oles) the Americans wouldn't leave. Oles thought the LTC had given in too easily, and now he understood why. It was a ploy. The ANA soldiers were incensed, glaring at him in hatred. They had been elated when they had learned of their departure minutes before. Now their commander informed them they were staying and put the blame on the Americans. The ANA all knew they were not to leave without the ETTs, who were now refusing to leave. It was becoming alarmingly tense again, just like it had the day of the IED.

The LTC came back over to the ETTs with his XO in tow. The LTC tried to reason with the Americans. He pointed out that the small task force had done their job. He added, "Already we have stayed in Nuristan two days longer than we were supposed to stay."

Furthermore, he reasoned, "It doesn't make any sense to stay, and it won't do any good to stay." Everyone knew he was speaking the truth, but then he added something the Americans knew to be dreadfully true. "The Afghan Police are angry at the continued American presence."

Both Oles and Longfield knew that was a big concern and had been from day one. It was getting increasingly difficult for the police to do their jobs and keep the status quo in the area. The ETTs knew the local ANP where the main reason they were still alive. Once the ANP turned on them, the game was over. They were dead men.

Longfield agreed with everything the LTC said—only, it didn't matter. They couldn't leave. They had been ordered to stay. Longfield listened as Oles said, "We are under orders. It's out of our hands. We can't leave Kamdesh."

The ANA officers were purple with rage.

The stress of command was starting to wear on Oles. The entire operation had been emotionally draining from day one and had never gotten better, only worse. Oles was dealing not only with the enemy, but also with his own inept high command, the bitter and oft irrational

ANA officers, the angry childish ANA soldiers, the unpredictable ANP, the seemingly two-faced local elders, and the responsibility and well-being of his own American soldiers—who were the only non-Muslims in the Province. In addition, there was the problem of Midwest, the lack of food, supplies, ammunition, and water, and the constant harassing fire from the enemy. Oles was exhausted in every way imaginable, dealing with problem after problem. He worried he would explode and struggled to keep his self-control.

On top of that, the Kamdesh elders had already complained several times about gunfire in the valley. It had been occurring daily since the Americans arrived. The elders were not happy and worried civilians would be injured or killed. When ACM on the cliffs fired, the ANA would return fire. Several times their PKM and AK rounds overshot the cliffs and landed near civilians almost a mile down the road. The Kamdesh elders wanted it to stop. Only the American departure would stop the gunfire.

Finally, after much discussion among themselves, the ANA officers exited the CP and issued orders to their men. The Americans followed them out but didn't need their Terps to understand. Higher ANA HQ and Americans be damned, the ANA were leaving. The LTC told his men to prepare for their departure. Oles didn't even try to stop them. After watching them for a moment, he walked back into the CP and sat down at the radio. Dejected, he called BDE.

"Saber 3, the ANA are leaving. There is nothing we can do about it. What are our orders?"

"The ANA are not to leave. You are to keep them there. Over."

"Saber 3," said Oles, not even fazed anymore, "repeat, the ANA are leaving. There is nothing we can do about it. What are our orders?"

"The ANA are not to leave. You are to keep them there. Over."

"Saber 3, repeat, the ANA are leaving. What are our orders?"

Pause.

Finally, after a long delay, a different officer got on the radio.

"(Omega 6), the ANA are not to leave. You are to keep them there. Over."

"Saber 3," said Oles, even though he knew it was not Saber 3 he was talking to, "the ANA are leaving. What are our orders?"

Another pause.

A longer one.

"*Well*," said the voice, finally, in defeat, "*if they leave, I guess you go with them.*"

"Saber 3," said Oles, "since they are leaving and we are to accompany them, what is the status on the comprehensive plan for our extraction?"

Silence.

Oles was so frustrated with the lack of answers from BDE and the incessant garbage they had fed him night after night that he finally said in disgust, "Don't worry. We are going to attack east. We will make our way out." What he wanted to say but didn't, was, "We sure as hell aren't going to rely on you assholes to get us out."

Longfield knew it was time to go. Not only were the ANA leaving, but the ANP were obviously livid at them for being in Kamdesh in the first place. The feeling of ill will was palpable. The ANA were leaving that night, and it was a good thing the Americans were told to go with them because Longfield doubted they would live much longer if they stayed. As it was, he worried they would get hit that day or on their way out that night.

No security patrol was sent out that day.

One last flaming raft was sent down the river that evening.

Oles called his four American NCOs together. In a few hours they were departing from what Oles referred to as "this hillbilly hellhole" of Afghanistan. They needed a security brief. This was a separate, independent briefing and only the Americans were present. Four of the five ETTs had come to terms with the fact that they might die on this mission. Even now, on the tail end of it, death looked more and more likely. Being a direct man, Oles talked candidly to his men.

"If you have to E-N-E (Escape and Evade), get the critical equipment. Any survivors need to burn us in the truck or throw us in the river. The last thing I want is to have my family see my dead body beheaded on CNN." He had said this before, but it was the time and place to reiterate the orders. He wasn't intentionally doing it to make Midwest blanch; it was what they all needed to hear. Oles watched the others nod in understanding, but poor Midwest looked like he was going to cry. It was strangely entertaining for Oles to watch Midwest when they talked about these morbid things, and it made Oles stress the danger and hopelessness of their circumstance all the more. Their situation was so upsetting to Midwest, it made the other four Americans talk about their deaths much more openly than they ever would have previously.

Midwest said something to Oles, but the CPT was so used to Midwest's whining he didn't even hear what the sergeant said. He thought, "You are just a big, sopping-wet pussy, aren't you?" Only, the way everyone looked wide-eyed at him after he said it made him turn to Dawson and say, "Did I just say that aloud?"

"Yes," said Dawson, "you did."

Dawson was trying unsuccessfully to keep a straight face and hide his mirth. Oles had gone off on Midwest many times about tactical stuff, but this was the first time he'd attacked the man's sense of courage. Oles expected the stocky sergeant to bristle with wrath but Midwest didn't appear to be in the least insulted by the statement and never let up with his whining.

Oles got back on the radio and talked to the SF for any last-minute instructions or help. He often wondered what they would have done without the SF. But the SF had nothing heartening for them—only, "Expect several contacts on your way out."

After speaking with his American soldiers, Oles briefed the ANA officers.

"We are going to leave in the early morning," he said, "around 0200. We will start infiltrating security forces to take control of key points along the road and search for IEDs." Oles hoped these security forces would discover and catch anyone who might be placing IEDs.

"As we pass each security force, that team will join up with us. It will be kind of like a route reconnaissance. We will use our mortars at every village we come to. Just like in Kamdesh, we'll pre-sight them on the ridges and give a little show of force, just in case." Oles knew that by registering the mortars and firing a couple of rounds near each village, his somewhat veiled threat would let anyone know that if he and his men got hit near a village, they were going to lob a bunch of 82mm rounds into it.

Then Oles deliberately told his ANA officers a lie. He did it because he knew they would immediately leak the information to the villagers (or their men would) after they left the briefing.

"We will have American B-52s and A-10s covering our egress. The B-52s will be so high the enemy will not be able to see them or hear them. The A-10s will be standing by at the closest base and be available to support us within minutes of making contact with the enemy." Oles had just told two of the biggest whoppers of his life. They had absolutely zilch in the way of support, but neither the ANA nor the bad guys knew that. The Taliban, al-Qaeda, Pakistanis, and foreign mercs had no reason not to believe the lies. In fact, A-10s had already appeared in the valley the day of the IED strike, so having the support was very plausible. Oles suspected the bad guys would hear all about their "CAS" within minutes of the briefings dismissal.

The village elders and many of the civilians who would help them walk out were invited to a going-away dinner. Before dusk they showed up and the ANA hosted a formal Afghan meal. Oles hoped the ANA had already leaked his ready air support information to them.

"Between putting out security forces, registering our mortars at each village, and doing some creative lying about ready air support, we were able to make it out. We all knew we were a cut hair away from having another *Blackhawk Down* story only the outcome wouldn't have been as successful."

Captain Marc Oles

EXTRACTION
September 25

The 0200 departure got pushed back several times until 0900. With over thirty Afghan villagers (including the Kamdesh village elder) walking in front of the vehicles, the American and ANA convoy of fifteen Toyota pickups and ten Ford Rangers rolled out of Kamdesh in single file, headed for Gowardesh. The IED-blasted truck was still drivable and it rolled out with the others. The twenty-five trucks were noticeably lighter and less crowded without the many MRE crates (over one thousand MREs were eaten during the stay) and ammunition boxes. They were leaving with fourteen fewer men than they had arrived with.

The villagers were hired by the local police (and paid for by the Americans) to walk the road in front of the vehicles in order to deter an attack—as the local warlords would obviously respond violently to any ACM or Taliban attack on their people. Using the metal detectors to check for IEDs and searching the ridges above as they moved, the convoy crept along at a snail's pace. Within 1,000 meters of their compound they found an IED buried in the road. It was perhaps 100 meters from where the first IED had exploded. They disabled it and continued on.

They had covered several kilometers without incident and approached one of the tiny hamlets along the road, nothing more than a few huts and buildings. Oles ordered the convoy to stop. He had Midwest's ANA weapons platoon register their mortars on the cliffs above the village and lob a few shells up on the rocks. The explosions were impressive, and Oles hoped they would get the point across. After firing the shells, the convoy continued on.

The procession traveled another mile and came across a second IED. They disabled it and the column kept snaking along the Nuristan Road with the locals still walking in front. At each village they stopped and registered their mortars. After the show of strength, they kept moving. In spite of the enemy's knowledge that they had mortars and a recoilless rifle, Oles was convinced it was the falsehood of air support that was allowing them to get out of Nuristan without being hit. Oles believed that when the ACM found out the small ANA detachment had air support, they figured it wasn't worth it to attack. They would be bombed by planes they couldn't see or hear. Also, if they hit the Americans, Coalition troops might come back in force.

The convoy spent the long day moving defensively, their eyes scanning the ridges above and their metal detectors checking the road in front. For intel purposes they took a few pictures of the terrain on the way out. It had been too dark to do so on the way in.

At dusk they rounded a bend in the mountains and approached the Saw Bridge at Gowardesh. The local villagers turned back and headed for home, leaving the convoy to continue on to Bari Kowt. They weren't home yet, but everyone was breathing easier.

When they neared Bari Kowt, they rounded another bend, and the men in the lead vehicle saw the SF waiting for them. Oles pulled up in his Ford Ranger and got out to talk to them. He noticed they actually looked happy to see him. And they were all laughing. Oles knew their laughter in itself was one hell of a complement. The SF had their own little community and didn't warm up to anyone. They never let outsiders in and especially not National Guard. Yet, here they were laughing and hollering good-naturedly at the guardsmen as they pulled up.

"Holy shit!" laughed one SF sergeant, "We didn't think we'd be seeing you guys ever again." The SF brought up the nightly communiqués with BDE and howled with laughter.

"The best was when you asked Saber 5 if Saber 4 or Saber 3 was in the CP. That was fuckin' hilarious." Oles and the others were also laughing. After days and days of stress, it was a marvelous release. They were finally safe.

"Now that it's over," admitted one of the SF operatives, "we're going to miss the nightly soap opera."

A view of the river on the way out

The Saw Bridge; Gowardesh – the last photo taken on the mission

Saturday September 24, 2005

Got a call today saying the mission was for 45 days prior & post election. If the ANA leaves tomorrow we'll be in hot water, even though it's been their mission from the start. The BC is asking for permission, but we are supposed to convince him to stay. The situation is getting critical, we split 38,000 Afghani between the 2 groups. And the locals don't like the ANA shooting at will. Everyone is pretty ragged, and latrine space is getting thin. We're ready to stay but need to get cold weather gear (via non existent resupply). MoD finally decided to go as planned. We're going to Barekowt then home. Tonite we're hosting all the people escorting us. Not good.

Sunday September 25, 2005

Got underway at 9 with people spread out all over including the politician – looks like the $50k and box of meds was worth it. Nothing happened until it came time to pay bills. WpnsCo gave a bill for 28 vehicles. Let's pay that, not so we told them all at 10am Mon pay line forms. Hruck Noo. For some reason 3rd Co is replacing 1st so Childress is awaiting all manner of problems.

SSG Dawson's journal entries for September 24 and 25

"I wish I had a better end to the story but at least we got out of there alive and none of us thought that would happen."

SFC Class Don Longfield

AFTERMATH

Oles's After Action Report was angry. Oles's BDE S-3 (Operations Officer) was also furious. Nobody knew what had happened and it was an extremely embarrassing mess when all the information about the mission was exposed. It was so bad that several 1st BDE officers were relieved within two months of Oles's return. On Christmas day, the commander of OMC-A (Office of Military Cooperation, Afghanistan), General James Hirai, came to talk to Oles about what had happened. Hirai was an American of Japanese descent and was, in Oles's opinion, a very impressive individual.[16]

"Yes," Oles remembered Hirai saying when Oles finished briefing him, "We dodged a bullet. It was fucked up, but like typical American soldiers throughout history, you pulled it out of your ass. Thanks."

What impressed Oles so much about Hirai was that he didn't come to apologize or try to make Oles and his men feel better. He came to find out what went wrong so he could fix the problem so that it wouldn't happen again. The problem was systemic, and if it wasn't addressed, it would be just a matter of time before some other unfortunate American soldiers were sent on another suicide mission. Hirai never wanted what Oles and his men experienced to happen again, and he took steps to ensure it didn't.

One of the results of the Kamdesh mission was a determination in the high command to avoid another situation like this one had been. Several times Longfield heard senior officers at a briefing say, "We will not do another Kamdesh," meaning they were not going to send people out without better support. Longfield took pride in the fact that their mission was successful. He also took satisfaction in the fact that their training had proven outstanding. Every wounded man had been saved by the ETTs' first-aid training. Longfield felt that he, Dawson, Strate, and Oles had performed to the highest standards of the US Army.

Coen was in Kabul when he ran into the ANA LTC who had brought the money to the ETTs at Bari Kowt. Coen didn't think much of the man and was convinced the Afghan had stolen thousands of US tax-payer's dollars. The ANA LTC saw Coen and, in typical Afghan fashion, greeted his American counterpart warmly. Coen embraced him and, feigning great concern, said, "I'm so glad to see you. I was worried about you."

The ANA officer didn't understand and asked, "Why?"

"Cuz I thought you'd be in jail by now. I thought you'd be in prison for taking all that money." Coen didn't know for sure which ANA officer had taken the cash, but he suspected the LTC. The Afghans next sentence told him everything he already supposed.

"Oh, I'll give the money back."

The money was never accounted for.

When they returned from Kamdesh they went to Mehtar-Lam. It was 2300, and they hadn't been there two hours when the base received mortar fire. Strate saw Marines, soldiers, and Air Force personnel running madly for the bunkers. Strate wasn't concerned at all. After Kamdesh, he felt this incoming was nothing. "Besides," he reasoned, "they aren't that damn accurate. If they hit the post, I'll be surprised." Instead of going to find cover, Strate went to check on his ANA.

Dawson returned to Kabul when it was time to rotate home. While occupied with archetypal hurry-up-and-wait Army procedure, he couldn't help but overhear some disconcerted officers complaining about how the base Dairy Queen was out of bananas, preventing them from having banana splits. Another was complaining about a recent lack of phone access to call home. Dawson shook his head and thought, "Hesco Hobbits…in the rear with the gear." He felt it was that type of lack of awareness for the soldier at the front that was harming the US efforts.

Longfield stayed in Asadabad, the only team member to do so. He was moved to Camp Joyce at Sarkani where he stayed for several months. Before he left to go back to the states, Longfield ran into two of the ANA soldiers he treated for wounds in Kamdesh. Private Hussein, the man with the "chicken bone" wound, lost his arm. He was manning a checkpoint in Jalalabad. The man with the leg wound now had a stump several inches above his missing knee. He walked with difficulty using crutches. Longfield noted that neither man was bitter about what had happened to him even though their future—and being able to provide for themselves—now looked very bleak.

Just as he was preparing to leave the country, Longfield ran into the colonel who had sent them on the mission. Longfield was loading his gear, and everyone he had initially flown in with was there, rotating out together. The colonel was the officer who had ordered, "Just get your ass in the truck and go!" Longfield heard he had been relieved of his command after Kamdesh. He hadn't seen him since.

Longfield walked over to him. "Sir, I have a question about Kamdesh for you."

"Okay. What do you got?"

"Did you actually give the order to, 'just get your ass in the truck and go'?" Longfield knew he had because he'd heard the order over the radio, but he wanted to hear it face to face.

"What are you talking about?"

"We were asking for medevac plans, close air support plans, re-supply plans, Ops orders, things like that. We had none of it. Did you actually give that order? 'Just get your ass in the truck and go!'"

"Well, you know, they were asking a lot of questions, and we really didn't have the answers." Longfield knew that was probably true—and the orders had come to the colonel from higher—but that still didn't make it right.

"That justifies telling us to get our asses in the truck and go?"

Silence.

No more was said and Longfield turned away. He got nothing but dirty looks from his former commander until he was discharged back at Fort Hood.

Oles was pulled from his team and taken back to Kabul to work on brigade staff. He knew the transfer had everything to do with the disastrous mission. He, Longfield, Dawson, Strate, and Midwest had been thrown to the wolves, but nobody wanted to talk about it. Oles didn't know, but he believed the order to execute came from the highest political levels. Whoever was directing couldn't afford to have the UN invalidate the entire parliamentary elections. That would have set Afghanistan's and the US/Coalition's goal for democracy back even further. But the truth of just how high it went may never be known. Whatever the source, it was more powerful than the Army. Everyone knew they had come within a "cut hair" to another Operation Redwing story.

As ridiculous as it was, the debacle mission was deemed a success. The ballots got out of Nuristan, and the politicians and newspapers proclaimed the mission a triumph for democracy. A scarce few American soldiers knew all the sordid details, but the operation itself turned out to be a good thing because there was tremendous fallout from the Kamdesh mission—so much so that it was really beneficial for forces following later. Everyone involved knew it stank to high heaven, but five Americans got lucky and, with typical American valor and tenacity, Oles, Dawson, Longfield, and Strate, pulled it off.[17] In his After Action Report, Oles praised the three sergeants for their professionalism and performance of duty. Of Midwest, Oles wrote, "He's had his fill."[18]

As for the soldiers who survived the Kamdesh debacle...

Strate finished his tour and rotated home to Indiana. He deployed to Iraq in 2008 and has since returned from that deployment. He is still in the Indiana National Guard.

Dawson was given a commander's coin for his part in the mission. When Dawson was told that higher-ups wanted to meet with them, he declined to go with Oles. He was too angry. Mohammad Rafiq and Mohammad Amin were his men. Dawson felt they were dead because of the stupidity of a few politicians and high-ranking officers. Mohammad Hussein had lost an arm. Another soldier had lost a leg. Others were wounded. Dawson felt all five ETTs could easily have died. Dawson was a soldier and willing to put his life on the line for his country but it was the way this mission had been conducted from the top that sickened him. He had obeyed orders in spite of it and had done everything asked of him but now that it was over he wanted no part of it or them. Dawson returned to Indianapolis and his day job. He left the National Guard.

Longfield returned to Oklahoma where he is now with his wife and children. He has suffered some permanent hearing loss from the mission (the RPG back-blast) in Kamdesh but not enough to keep him from active duty. He is now a 1st Sergeant and has returned from a January, 2008 deployment to Iraq.[19]

Sergeant Midwest, according to Strate, has since retired from the Army National Guard.

Oles deployed to Iraq in December, 2007. He returned in January 2009 and is presently back in Indiana with his wife and family.

Several months after Kamdesh, in late 2005, Oles was in Kabul working at his new job when he ran into some SF operatives. They had just come in from the field. These men had been working on the southwestern side of Afghanistan along the Iranian border, hundreds and hundreds of kilometers from Nuristan. Because of the Kamdesh fiasco, Oles had a great appreciation for SF and went out of his way to always thank them. He explained to these guys that it was SF in Naray who had helped them out of a tight spot when they were in Kamdesh.

"Holy shit!" said one of the operatives. "Were you one of those fuckers they left hanging out in Nuristan?" The soldier explained that he, too, was monitoring their radio broadcasts from all the way on the other side of Afghanistan. "Dude," he said to Oles, "that was fucked up!"

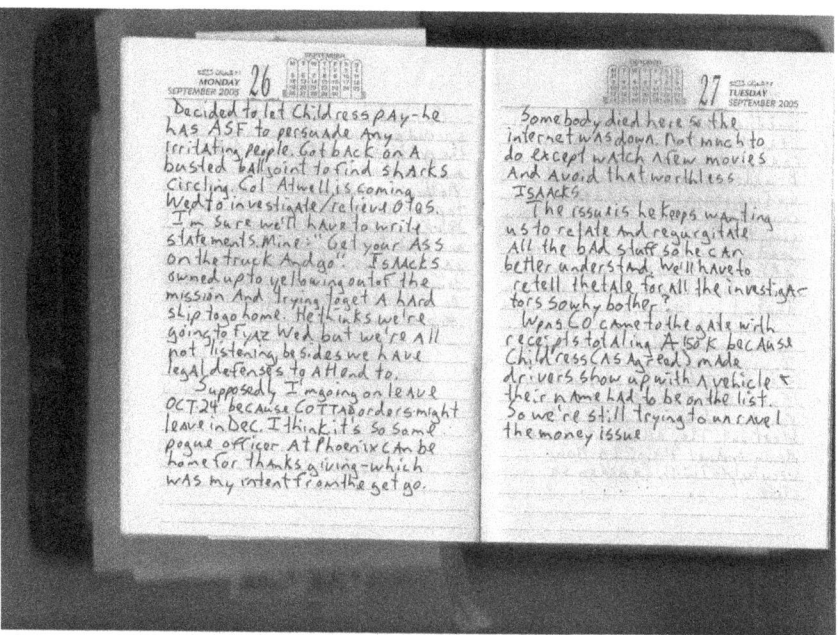

SSG Dawson's journal entries for September 26 and 27

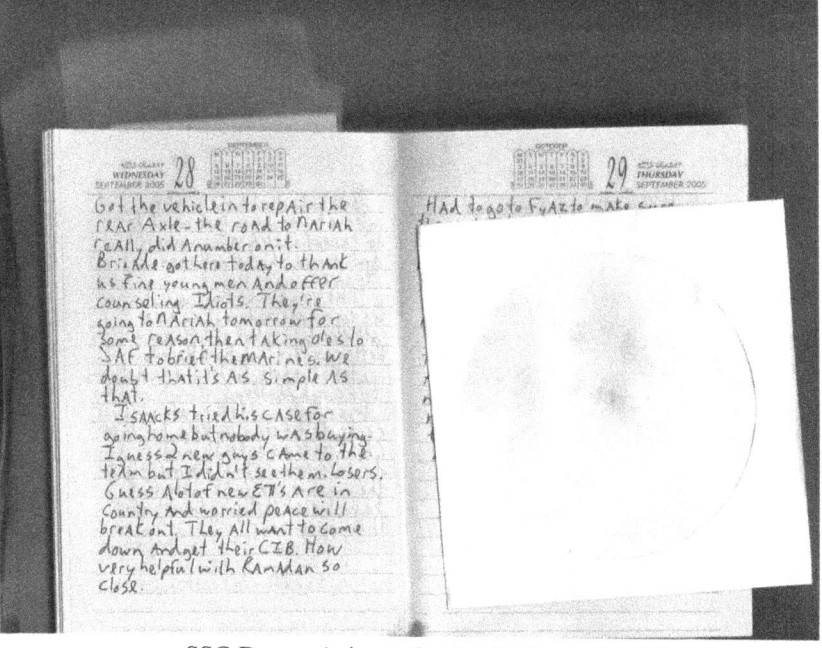

SSG Dawson's journal entry for September 28.

Books by James F. Christ

Afghanistan War Series:

The Bone Yard	October 12, 2003
Morghab Canyon	July 29, 2004
Kamdesh	September 16-25, 2005
Landigal	August 3, 2006
Shudergay	July 24, 2006

World War Two

Mission Raise Hell	October 28-Nov 4, 1943
Battalion of the Damned	August 7-September 14, 1942
Iwo; Assault on Hell	February 19-March 27, 1945
Memories from Tuskegee	Life story of LTC C. C. Jamison

[1] "Midwest" is a pseudonym. The E-7s real name is withheld.

[2] A Tasker is a document directed at assigning certain elements of the Phoenix and BDE Headquarters with specific tasks that would enable the soldiers involved in the operation to accomplish their mission

[3] Oles's paternal grandfather had come to the US as a German prisoner of war during WWI. His paternal grandmother was killed in Germany during a bombing raid in WWII.

[4] LTC Coen said the exact same thing about the US Marines/Marine doctrine, and the superior professionalism of the Marines. "Very true," offered Coen, in his interview. "Saw it all the time." SSG Combes shared this sentiment.

[5] Dawson, in anger, was referencing the famous quote by Marcus Flavinus: "We had been told, on leaving our native soil, that we were going to defend the sacred rights conferred on us by our ancestors' toil and sacrifice and to bring benefits to populations in need of our assistance and our civilization.

We were able to verify that all this was true, and, because it was true, we did not hesitate to shed our quota of blood, to sacrifice our youth and our hopes. We regretted nothing, but whereas we over here are inspired by this frame of mind, I am told that in Rome factions and conspiracies are rife, that treachery flourishes, and that many people in their uncertainty and confusion lend a ready ear to the dire temptations of relinquishment and vilify our action.

I cannot believe that all this is true, and yet recent wars have shown how pernicious such a state of mind could be and to where it could lead. Make haste to reassure me, I beg you, and tell me that our fellow-citizens understand us, support us and protect us as we ourselves are protecting the glory of Rome.

If it should be otherwise, if we should have to leave our bleached bones on these desert sands in vain, then beware of the anger of the Legions!" Marcus Flavinus, Centurion, 2nd Cohort, Augustan Legion.

[6] Said Dawson, "Title 10 was operational funds-"OPFunds". Op Funds were for incidentals like roadside tire repair, requiring a receipt. Payfunds came monthly. During the Foo/pay briefing we were told to "spend OPFunds like it's your money" if remaining funds didn't match receipts spent there could have been repayment from my paycheck, court martial, possible prison time. This money was outside of all those requirements, a would-be unreported bribe."

[7] "You will be hearing more and more about that road in the months and year to come," said Oles during his 2006 interview. "Especially now that 10th Mountain is pushing so hard up there."

[8] The Toyota Hilux pickup was brought to Afghanistan in mass after the US occupation and distributed to civilians.
[9] Nienhaus, Michael C.
Subject: US/UK Counter Narcotics Strategy Mwwrinf 22-23 January 2007
US/UK Counter Narcotics Strategy Meeting
22-23 January 2007
State Department Headquarters. Notes Summery: These notes are "Sensitive but Unclassified"
[10] Oles received this information from the SF upon return to Naray after the mission. They explained to him that after that second contact, they figured the Guardsmen were dead men.
[11] In his 2006 interview, Oles used the word "half-assed" to describe the job.
[12] In his interview, Don Longfield said, "You sit through all this combat lifesaver fuckin' medical training, you say not again, but when it's done, if you ever need it, you are damn glad you sat through all that bullshit medical training. The Army does prepare you. You are able to do it without thinking about it. You look at a wound and you are able to treat it. It's automatic. We had everything but a sucking chest wound and we were able to treat it."
[13] AFGHANISTAN: SUCCESSFUL AFGHAN ELECTIONS PROVE CRITICS WRONG, RUMSFELD SAYS
Posted 9/21/2005 9:19:23
By Sgt. Sara Wood, USA
American Forces Press Service
[14] This conversation/discussion was recreated from the interviews of Longfield and Oles and approved by Strate and Dawson.
[15] AFGHANISTAN: BUSH: Afghanistan proof of progress in war on Terror.
Posted 9/23/2005 9:17:17
By Sgt. Sara Wood, USA
American Forces Press Service
[16] Hirai served as commander of U.S. Army Alaska; chief of staff U.S. Army Pacific; commander of the U. S. Army Garrison, Hawaii; commander of the 3rd Battalion, 21st Infantry, 25th Infantry Division (Light); and two tours on the Commander U.S. Pacific Command staff. He also served as Deputy Commandant, U. S. Army Command and General Staff College, Fort Leavenworth, Kansas and six years with the US Army Rangers. His career included tours in Washington, Texas, Kentucky, and Germany as an infantryman in Air Assault, Airborne Ranger, Mechanized and Light units.

A graduate of the University of Hawaii with a master's in education from Troy State University, he is a graduate of the Infantry Officers Basic and Advanced Courses, Armed Forces Staff College and the U.S. Army War College.

He has received the Distinguished Service Medal, Defense Superior Service Medal, Legion of Merit fifth award, Bronze Star Medal, Defense Meritorious Service Medal, Expert Infantryman Badge, Master Parachutist Badge, Air Assault Badge and the Ranger Tab.

After retiring from active duty in the U.S. Army, Hirai joined APCSS in April 2006. As the special assistant to the Commander, Combined Forces Command – Afghanistan, he worked in the Office of Security Cooperation - Afghanistan leading the external support to the Afghan Ministry of Defense and National Army.

[17] Oles, a former Marine, felt that the entire operation would have been different, with a much more successful outcome and far fewer problems, had Marines been involved in the operation.

[18] "He was useless in every way," said Oles. Strate said this of Midwest: Personally, he's a good guy. But he's not a soldier. That's what it boils down to. From a soldier's perspective he just needs to get the hell out of the military and get on with his life.

[19] "You know, I volunteered to go back to Afghanistan. I believe in the U.S. mission so much that I'm willing to make the sacrifice. I'm not sure, but it seems to me that the law of averages will catch up to a soldier. You are not going to keep being so fuckin' lucky." Sergeant First Class Don Longfield.

www.ingramcontent.com/pod-product-compliance
Lightning Source LLC
Chambersburg PA
CBHW051757040426
42446CB00007B/411